# PRETTY UGLY

## More Oxymorons & Other Illogical Expressions
## That Make Absolute Sense

# Warren S. Blumenfeld, Ph.D.

Illustrated by Lisa Amoroso

A PERIGEE BOOK

Perigee Books
are published by
The Putnam Publishing Group
200 Madison Avenue
New York, NY 10016

Library of Congress Cataloging-in-Publication Data

Blumenfeld, Warren S.
    Pretty ugly: more oxymorons and other illogical expressions that make
absolute sense / by Warren S. Blumenfeld; illustrated by Lisa
Amoroso.—1st American ed.
        p.  cm.
    ISBN 0-399-51493-7
    1. Oxymoron—Humor.  2. Pleonasm—Humor.  3. American wit and
humor.  4. English language—Terms and phrases—Humor.  I. Amoroso,
Lisa.  II. Title.
    PN6231.098B58     1989          88-15192 CIP
    428.1′0207—dc19

Printed in the United States of America
1  2  3  4  5  6  7  8  9  10

# Acknowledgments:
## Heroes, Unsung and Sung

DEAN OF OXYMORON'S WARNING:

Oxymorons (And Now Pleonasms) Still Continue
To Be Addictive, Cause Laughter, And Certainly
May Complicate Pregnancy

As with *Jumbo Shrimp*, it would be easier to acknowledge those incredibly few, but tremendously small, people who didn't encourage me; but that would be oxymoronic logic. Rather, let me again attempt the more difficult, albeit the more pleasant—to acknowledge, with genuine appreciation, the so many who *did* encourage me, *did* make positive contributions:

All those cited in *Jumbo Shrimp*. I meant it then; I mean it now. Let me especially repeat:

Steven Kutner, David Hein, Herbert Kaufman, and Norman Sanders (all of whom kept me, and still continue to keep me, in the game).

Several people I never met and whose names I'll never know (two of whom are in my sight at all times).

Milton Blood (who put me in the oxymoron closet originally).

David Snell, Vickie York, Herschel Brown, Billy Bowles, Mark Donovan, and Adrienne Ingrum (all of whom brought me out of the oxymoron closet—even if only on a permanently temporary basis—and the last, but not the least, of whom forced me not only to learn but also to grow. [She is not forgiven.])

Josh Blumenfeld and Esther Blumenfeld (both of whom put up with, and continue to put up with, this important trivia long before it was either and now that it is neither).

And let me add:

*Jumbo Shrimp* readers, as well as radio call-in addictees (so many of whom reaffirmed it was indeed a crowded, albeit cavernous, closet).

Carey Bynum (who suggested this before either one of us was listening), as well as Brian Hayes (who used the *Jumbo Shrimp* mailer to make a similar suggestion).

Peter Van Dusen and Alix Kanegy (for their respective roles in the creation(s) of Jumbo Shrimp Blumenfeld and Colossal Shrimp Blumenfeld, disrespectfully).

Noah Adams, Ernie Allen, Robert Armstrong, Harold Balske, John Berkeley, Bill Bishop, Jim Bohannon, Neal Boortz, Peter Boyles, David Brudnoy, Katy Caraway, Sandra Carnet, Ginger Carter, Joe Collins, Paul Crawley, Mills Crenshaw, Kathy Cronkite, Maxine Crooks, Mike Dale, Kim Day, John Delle Monache, Gale Dick, Art Dineen, Gary Dodge, Paul Dunn, John Eastman, Sharon Ellis, Lee Fowler, Frances Franklin, John Fredrickson, Jim French, Peter Fullam, Scott Gagel, John Gambling, Marlene Gerson, Donna Gillmor, Joe Goodman, Bruce Gordon, Glenn Haig, Elizabeth Hartigan, Ed Hartley, Richard Hayes, Kenny Hazelett, Wayne Herman, Tom Hopkins, Tom Isham, Tom Jensen, Lisa Johnson, Tom Johnson, Tony Johnson, Donald Johnston, Rob Johnston, Brice Keegan, J Michael Kenyon, Audree Koenigsberg, Paul Landino, Jimmy Launce, Dianne Laursen, Anne Lawson-Beerman, Bob Lee, J. P. McCarthy, Mike McConnell, Nancy McDaniel, Gary McKee, Perry Marshall, Cyndee Maxwell, Mike Meenan, Pete Michaud, Jan Mickelson, Craig Mollison, Pat Morell, Bunny Morse, Paul Muchinsky, Anton Mueller, Carolyn Mungo, Mike Murphy, Susan Murphy, Mark Murray, Ernie Myers, Lisa Nicholas, Dan Nilsen, Roy Norris, John Oakley, Don O'Briant, Kerry O'Brien, Elle Pankin, Dan Parker, Bob Pavolovich, Clarence Petersen, Chuck Podhaisky, Larry Powell, Pam Pryor, Stacy Reish, Jim Reyland, Bryan

Rhodes, Bob Riggins, Jaine Rodack, Pat Rodgers, Mike Rosen, Antonia Ruiz, Dave Scott, Mike Scott, Don Silverman, Eliza Sonneland, Dennis Sullivan, John Swaney, Arn Tibbitt, Gay Totten, Don Vogel, John Wark, Tom Webb, Kathy West, Melanie Woods, and Mel Young (all of whom contributed to the visibility of *Jumbo Shrimp* and oxymorons—thereby contributing to the current pretty ugly product).

Burton Gruber (my personable accountant, who not only makes housecalls but also delivers oxymorons).

Paul Kquia, for his edited-out, at the last second, story of how an oxymoron changed a man's life in Delaware a few years ago. Sorry, Paul.

The former current copy editor, Anna Jardine, for whose nervous breakdown I fairly sincerely apologize, and in spite of whom I seem to have broken all the rules of style and grammar—again, many intentionally, and with limited impunity.

Lisa Amoroso, once again, whose patience is exceeded only by her artistic talent.

. . . and a special thanks to Charlie de Kay for his professional kid gloves.

And finally again, people who write, read, speak, and/or listen . . . and college students and/or teenagers (again for obscurely obvious but now logical reasons).

Finally, yet once again, all are very extremely unique—but in the same identical way. Once again, if I inadvertently left anyone out, it was only because I meant to and/or we had to save a few pages for the product, pretty ugly though it may be.

# Dedication:
## Qualified Sincerity, Truly Sincere

Again, to myself, without whom I definitely probably might never have done whatever it is I seem to have done here again.

And again, in addition, however, to my mother (from whence cometh my sense of humor, such as it is), who still continues to be both funny and a lady. Ergo therefore, hi, Mom.

Again also, hi, Esther and/or Josh.

And again, also too, to Mrs. Richardson, who still continues to demonstrate old age can be an oxymoron rather than a pleonasm.

Thanks, all; you deserve better—perhaps even outstanding excellence . . . maybe next time.

# Contents:
## Random Organization: Sequential Order

Faculty Meeting

**Faculty cooperation**

# Introduction:
## Déjà Vu Remembered, Sort of

I've been working on a terrific foolproof get-rich-quick scheme now for about thirty years . . . and getting closer with each passing decade. (Incidentally, this is not it—yet.)

However, and having a lot less to do with that than I would prefer, if you are the one who missed the beginning of all this oxymoron business, not to worry, here we go again. (But I warn you now: Once you start, there is no stopping; there is no way out—no escape. It is not unlike sliding down a razor blade—albeit a tad more [or less] pleasant—at least at first. Ask any of the addicted masses, huddling to be free. Posted; fair warning.)

Given as I am to bombastic understatement, in *Jumbo Shrimp* I semiaccurately reported oxymorons had destroyed my life. That was the good news. It got worse!

Since then, Dickens (and his oxymoronic opening to *A Tale of Two Cities*) has been right. It has been the best of times; it has been the worst of times. (But how in the dickens could Dickens have known?) I refer, of course, to my so-called life since publication of my so-called *Jumbo Shrimp & Other Almost Perfect Oxymorons*. What else would you call it?

Do I have your attention? I said, do I have your attention? Notwithstanding, the rest of you, follow me. Walk (and/or talk/listen) this way.

For those of you who may have been out of town, let me review the bidding. In that 1986 semidefinitive mini-epic instant classic, as reported above, I indicated I was never sure whether I needed to define or defend oxymorons. Now, fourteen months later, I am even positively less sure than before. On the off chance you missed my initial fall from grace, let me catch you up (said the spider to the fly).

Therefore, fully aware of the possibility of insulting at least one group of readers—although

I'm not sure which, the group that did read *Jumbo Shrimp*, or the group that did not—let me begin with definition and pronunciation.

## Definition: Broad and Otherwise

Therefore, if you know what an oxymoron is, please raise your hand—or at least an eyebrow. Minimally, blink twice . . . or exhale, don't just recline there! Aha! Just as I thought, perfect ambiguity. Therefore, let me begin again. Please pay particular partial attention.

An oxymoron is two concepts (usually two words) that do *not* go together but are used together. It is the bringing together of contradictory expressions. Consider, yet again, jumbo shrimp (yet again, please!), freezer burn, even odds, divorce court, near miss, cardinal sin, good loser, slightly pregnant, Amtrak schedule, civil war, and clean dirt.

You may also vaguely recall it was I—or maybe even me—who suggested oxymorons were addictive. (Why else would you be back again, even if for only the first time, and/or why else would I be back again, also even if for only the first time?) Further, they were ubiquitous, insidious, and being increasingly used by, among others, those who write and/or speak, in a veiled apparent attempt to say everything to everybody that ends up saying nothing to anybody—however eloquently. Got that? Good; way to got!

## Pronunciation: Watch My Lips

It (still) usually embarrasses me that I almost always mispronounce the word "oxymoron." This is particularly so inasmuch as I have now been accorded the minor honor of being the world's oxymoron expert (a title I continue to accept with either arrogant humility or humble arrogance—

I haven't decided which yet. And besides, no one else wants the title—or, more accurately in this case, the subtitle).

Anyway, here's the straight subterfuge: You can pronounce "oxymoron" any way you want—as long as you don't mispronounce it. It is still pronounced roughly the way it looks and sounds—although I occasionally get strangely accented love-hate mail from antepenultimists. How many of you looked it up *(antepenultimist* or *oxymoron)* last time? This time? Next time? Serves you right!

## On Becoming Addicted: An Even Briefer Odyssey

Last time we talked, I related to you, in gross detail, a brief odyssey of how I became addicted. I insincerely meant almost every word of it. After all, have I ever lied to you before? In that complete partial accounting, I secretly exposed such oxymorons as vaguely aware, definitely probably, justifiably paranoid, almost suddenly, completely educated, completed research, standard deviation, management science, marketing research, first annual, first deadline, certainly unsure, cavalier concern, almost candid, insincere vow, science fiction, glacierlike rapidity, almost totally, perhaps predictably, talk show, live television, local network, resolute ambivalence, three originals, original copy, minor moment, positively grudgingly, and political promise, among others (or, for you frequent-flying foreign airline devotees, *inter alia).*

In terms of the exquisite pain of it all, I felt very much the semiperfect idiot savant. Further, the (then) response to my oxymoronic activities was characterized by having moved with deliberate speed from intense apathy (oooh, I like that kind of talk!) to mild interest to partial success to controlled enthusiasm, finally even approaching qualified success.

## True Oxymorons Versus Quasi Oxymorons

Oh yes, not unlike greatness (even minor greatness), a semidistinction between true and quasi oxymorons was thrust upon you. A true oxymoron is a contradiction in a natural state, independent of personal values. Examples of trues were (and still are) almost perfect, and fast food.

A quasi oxymoron, on the other hand, by definition, is not a true oxymoron. (Again, why didn't you think of that? Stay alert; the pace is picking up.) It is characterized by personal values and, perhaps best or worst of all, depending upon one's values, includes an element of sarcasm. Right or right, the example that usually springs to mind first for most folks is military intelligence—or mayhap you prefer legal brief, Texas chic, faculty cooperation, sophisticated New Yorker, educational administration, or compassionate editor. It was also suggested quasis were most people's favorites, but I liked them anyway (quasis—not most people). Finally again, it was indicated (as opposed to contra-indicated) that if you had a problem distinguishing trues and quasis, you were probably—but not necessarily—human. Does any of this sound familiar? But to whom?

## Oxymoron Sources: Obvious Secret Hiding Places

Oxymoron sources were then indicated, suggesting oxymorons are to be found everywhere (occasionally intentionally), but some places were better sources than others. With slight qualification, it was strongly recommended you search out situations where people write, read, speak, and/or listen, and suggested you forget about other, less productive situations. As a matter of fact, my initial final conclusion and explicitly ambiguous recommendation was that you should search out oxymorons from life, or if that were too restrictive, look elsewhere (which, judging from the mail—much of which was unsent—many of you did). Good advice then, good advice now. Remember, you heard it here.

## Chaotic Organization: Perfect Misfit

Finally—or is it finally again? I certainly think we passed finally several finalies back—I described the chaotic organization of the book and requested (for our mutual mental hygiene) that we share oxymorons. A mailer was provided—roughly on page 95, paragraph 1ff. I indicated my intention to include reader (and even reader writer) contributions in future oxymoron books (assuming the initial book got published—which I now am given to understand it was ... although I think Putnam/Perigee demonstrated something less than total confidence by issuing the first 50,000 books in No. 2 pencil).

I anticipate partly making good on that commitment within the current covers—or is it sheets? Anyway, finally again (see how that works?), I passively tried to warn you oxymorons had almost absolutely no socially redeeming quality except that they make people smile out loud and are

**Completely educated**

addictive—but not necessarily habit-forming, or in that order. And then, finally once again (I don't know about you, but I can't take much more of this!), I stated they were *not* for everyone—only people who write, read, speak, and/or listen . . . and college students and/or teenagers. But you know all of this, have all the prerequisites. It's all sorta like coming home, isn't it? . . . to the wrong house. Why else would you be back? Hey, where are you going?

**Live television**

### The Passive Challenge on Page 22 of *Jumbo Shrimp*

Also recall the verbal *shrimp* gauntlet that was hurled, in terms of your identifying the actual number of oxymorons in *Jumbo*, allowing (a) there were approximately 1,231 oxymorons; (II) absolutely no recognition would be given to the astute reader who identified all—or even more than all—the oxymorons; and (3) no approximate solution—or even exact account—would ever be made available. You were then encouraged to sleep well (which apparently most of you did).

Contrary to (a), (II), and (3) above, although it's probably not a sincere lie, I wish to report that four people (from five different cities) came up with the correct solution. Unfortunately, it was not the same correct solution—and I seem to have misplaced their names (but you know who you are; be proud and/or happy in your work).

## Planned Serendipity or Chance Goals: Unachievable Accomplishments

Little or no doubt you've been wondering what's happened with and/or to me since *Jumbo Shrimp*. For example, in regard to the immediate goals stated on page 93 of that book. For now, to be completely succinct in depth, well, uh, yes and no, sort of, almost exactly sort of, almost exactly, or perhaps a firm maybe will suffice—but not necessarily in that order. And that's but a whole part of what I want to talk with you about in this second first annual oxymoron book (we're just going to have to keep doing it until I get it right). But, and this may be somewhat earth-shaking, in addition, a new dragon has surfaced—and the name is not Puff; the name is Pleonasm—but more on that (the P word) later . . . very much later.

And seemingly perhaps even more important, did I become the consummate ultimate antepenultimist? Or, failing that, did I become the consummate ultimate anti-antepenultimist? Well, sadly, perhaps predictably, it turns out I did not; either. (But I'm still trying . . . very. Just ask my friends, either of them.) Perhaps not unlike you, I was mispronouncing the word. But how can one be sure? Besides, I spoke with a midwestern southern accent. You think that's easy? Actually, easier done than said.

Pleonasms? Oh yeah, I'm getting to them, I'm getting to them, I'm getting to them. **15**

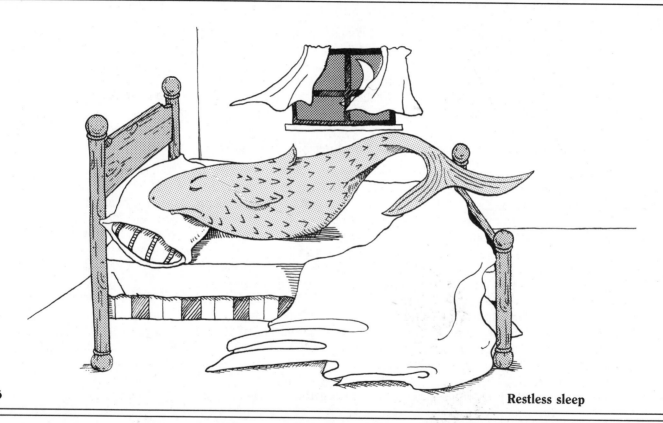

Restless sleep

# Purpose and Organization:
# You Can Get Here from There

As you both no doubt vaguely recall, the single purpose of that first annual oxymoron book was to describe the ubiquitous and insidious nature of oxymorons, to raise your awareness level about oxymorons, to infect and/or addict you, to RUIN YOUR LIFE just as mine had been somewhat destroyed. Toward accomplishing this ruination and destruction, four points (remember? remember? remember? and remember? . . . and in that order) were addressed toward inducing said mass oxymoron addiction (just say yes). That is still at least half (and the larger half at that) of my single goal regarding this second first annual oxymoron book. As a matter of fact, I've already done it. So there!

The other half, actually really the equal half, is to describe the ubiquitous and insidious nature of yet another small trivial unimportant semantic phenomenon (if you guessed pleonasms, you guessed it, but don't tell the person seated next to you on your extreme right—at least not yet); to raise your awareness level about this most recent latest unhealthy sickness of mine; to infect and/or addict you; to still continue to again RUIN YOUR LIFE, again.

### The Initial Element in the Perfect Misfit

Last time, I went through exquisite pain to point out to you, dear reader (yeah, you), how things were loosely organized. That worked so well that this time I think I'll just let you figure it out yourself. Trust me on this one. So much for one trial learning.

Toward accomplishing these somewhat imminently worthy goals, what (I think) will happen along the way is that I'll report on some of *your* contributed oxymorons (you *did* contribute, didn't you? You *don't* want to be left out, do you?); catch you up on some oxymoronic current events; give you my current all-time top-ten list of oxymorons; and tell you what's been happening with me oxymoronically. Hey, what are fiends for?

### The Second Important Critical Element in the Exactly Perfect Plan

Then I'll freely self-admit how one bad habit can beget (and did indeed begot) another—demonstrating that no bad deed goes unrewarded (or is it "No good deed goes unpunished"?), showing you how one semantic addiction led to another. If you guessed pleonasms *again*, you are exactly correct again (but ahead of your time, as well as this book's schedule—so cool it!). Toward that end, I will indicate how a free gift cost me dearly, in the process giving definitions of the problem. Then, having learned my lessons the first time, rather than try to make my task easier and yours more difficult, I will systematically organize the material into three independent, but discrete, categories. These three discrete, but independent, categories will be Miscellaneous pleonasms, Other pleonasms, and Unclassified pleonasms (can you handle it?). For those who survive the long march, I will also reveal publicly my enduring all-time permanent top-ten list of pleonasms. An added feature this time *may* be some progress measures of your ability proficiency to understand and/or comprehend (I haven't decided definitely yet).

### Then an Expected Planned Unexpected Surprise: On the Level

Then (my editor thinks) the plan calls for the appearance of a special mystery guest word, *if* I can come up with one. There's no rush, it's only noon; I have plenty of time, i.e., fifty-seven pages. Ah, ah, ah . . . no peeking. Aha; and certainly no guessing.

### Opposites Attract Opposites: Contradictions Contradict Contradictions and Coexist, Almost

You thought that being monocursed with oxymorons was tough? Patiently wait. Either before or after (but definitely not during) that expected planned unexpected surprise (on the level), and either in a fit of peake or at the peak of fit, I will give you a semi-idea of how difficult it is to coexist with the (now) dual curse of oxymorons *and* pleonasms, suggesting restless sleep (certainly not TV) may be the only escape. For now, let's just sleep on that one. Later . . .

### All's Well That Ends

And then, in initial conclusion (or final conclusion, depending on whether you end up being an oxymoron addict or a pleonasm addict—you choose it, or it will choose you; just hope it's not both [heh, heh, heh]), I will tie all this together in a single disjointed package and/or one whole totality. Perhaps not unlike you, I patiently can't wait to see how this all ends, to hear what I have to say (I said, to hear what I have to say).

### Request for Oxymoronic and/or Pleonastic Contributions

Once again, henceforth and/or forevermore (or 20,000 miles, whichever comes first), you will find oxymorons (and now pleonasms) impossible, but not difficult, to avoid. Stepping nimbly to one side will step you into either one or the other; and there's no turning back (you already have begun the long slide). So wear old shoes—semantically speaking.

Ubiquity (which seemingly is everywhere) raises its ugly head, yet once again. Therefore, I again recommend an outlet. See page 95.

Once again, if your oxymoron is old news, well and good, and insincere thanks. But if it is a find, even better, and less sincere thanks. On the other hand, if your pleonasm is a new innovation, very well and extremely good, and really sincere appreciation. And if it is a newer-than-new find, even extremely better, and much more sincere appreciation.

In either case, please be sure to include your source. I intend to include your withheld contributions, as well as your donated contributions, in the next last generation of future oxymoron and/or pleonasm books. (Once again, this assumes *this* book gets published, a condition the first initial book did not totally satisfy. I mean, No. 2 pencil? And printed on the backs of old office memos?)

## Warning: Now Listen Up, and Listen Up Tight

Oxymorons and pleonasms are addictive (just say maybe, firmly).

But also too, and not so incidentally, in *Jumbo Shrimp*, we (read: editor) took the device of putting most—but not all—of the oxymorons in boldface. We received mixed reactions about that particular print ploy. About half of you liked it; about half of you didn't like it; and the plurality of you displayed extreme intense apathy (although it's not too late to be heard from, or, for you purists, from whom to be heard).

Therefore, this time, we (again, read editor) have decided to put *everything* in boldface (*or* to put *nothing* in boldface, depending upon whether you bought Form A or Form B of *Pretty Ugly*). Therefore, in a sense (if indeed there is any sense to any of this), you're on your own. With that in mind (yours, not mine), I will partially leave you to work through the book by yourself at this point. However, I'll be partially back later. I'll meet you again on page 89. For those afraid to tramp through the oxymoronic/pleonastic/palindromic (oops—and/or aha—I told!) woods by yourselves, you can now move immediately to page 89 right now; and I'll literally hold your hand, figuratively.

# 2 The *Jumbo Shrimp* Readers Write: Insomniacs, Arise!

You may recall there was a mechanism (a mailer) on page 95 of *Jumbo Shrimp* with which you could vent your semantic spleen, get even with me for keeping you awake nights with oxymorons—although I do appreciate the thank-you notes from all the narcoleptics (many of whom were my students). Many addictees, having had enough, not being able to stand it any longer, did indeed grasp pen between thumb and forefinger and got even with me (or whomsoever) via the mailer. While I cannot list all the submissions received, nor can I say they were necessarily original or did not appear in *Jumbo Shrimp* or do not appear in the present whatever-this-is, I sorta really appreciate the effort very much. Further, legal constraints may prohibit me from naming names; ergo, I may have used initials (yes, first initials).

Much of the mail was quasi hate—along the lines of "You rotten person, you and/or your damn oxymorons are keeping me up nights." I don't suppose you'd believe me if I told you the letter came from Johnny Carson? How 'bout David Letterman? I didn't think so.

I even got a piece of pure hate mail. That's the good news—the bad news is that it was postmarked from Atlanta and the handwriting looked suspiciously like that of one member of my family who shall go nameless (probably the nameless one who can write—as opposed to read. Hey, you can't please everyone! But the family that preys together . . . ).

Also, you should be aware there were many duplications (multiple originals?), such that giving exact credit (or is it discredit?) is an impossible possibility. Where ties (or closer) occurred, I tried to use postmark dates. Therefore, just kinda lay back, let the oxymoronic waves wash over you, and enjoy. Following is something less than a population of the samples.

| | | |
|---|---|---|
| vexation exercise | Jeff Ashworth | Atlanta, GA |
| good lawyer | C. E. Neubauer | West Palm Beach, FL |
| regional pantheists | Dennis Sullivan | Atlanta, GA |
| plastic canvas | Richard Koch | San Diego, CA |
| aching joys | Cherian S. Thackenkary | Atlanta, GA |
| practical joke | Barbara R. Sistrunk | Southfield, MI |
| sugarless candy | Dotty Cooly | West Harwich, MA |
| water landing | Gary Dodge | Denver, CO |
| fake fur | Eugene F. Reiner | St. Paul, MN |
| oversized brief | Louis B. Gorman | Phoenix, AZ |
| sweet pickle | Addis Gutmann | Seattle, WA |

**Fake fur**

| | | |
|---|---|---|
| mildly psychotic | Kenneth L. Stoner | Lawrence, KS |
| creation science | Brian Hayes | Fort Lewis, WA |
| entertaining sermon | Julie O'Connor | Albany, NY |
| young Republicans | James R. Holton | Seattle, WA |
| whole half | Eleanore Eldrige | Lake Worth, FL |
| tax-free | Leonard G. Lorch | Stanford, CA |
| budget gourmet | Alyce Hirschi | Chicago, IL |
| cold toast | Ken Douglass | Baltimore, MD |
| congressional action | Robert Gordon | San Luis Obispo, CA |
| motorcycle safety | Elsa H. Sagasti | Arlington, VA |
| wealthy professor | Clyde W. Faulkner | Atlanta, GA |
| Justice Rehnquist | Frank J. Nivert | Fort Myers, FL |
| traditionally radical | Franz Dovsky | Mount Carmel, CT |
| *Humane Robotics* | Paul Mills | Knoxville, TN |
| loose tights | Bert W. Beecher | Indianapolis, IN |
| near miss | Jody Fowler | Fremont, CA |
| dull shine | Mrs. Blumenfeld (hi, hon) | Lake Worth, FL |
| Long Island Expressway | WYNY listeners | New York, NY |
| Harvard-educated | Al Roberts | Atlanta, GA |
| semiboneless ham | Marjorie Glazer | Shrewsbury, MA |
| benevolent despot | Melissa J. Nirenberg | New Haven, CT |
| commercial art | Stephen G. Scolmanini | San Jose, CA |
| San Jose, IL | Barbara Appel | Galesburg, IL |

| | | |
|---|---|---|
| deaf piano tuner | The Blees family (of piano tuners) | Webster Groves, MO |
| Orioles victory | Anonymous baseball fan | Baltimore, MD |
| superette | Phillip M. Cohen | Aliquippa, PA |
| silent testimony | William C. Wilson | Douglasville, GA |
| safe sex | Joyce Slater | Kennesaw, GA |
| accidentally on purpose | Michelle Mahonin | Bernardsville, NJ |
| eternal life | Jen Weisberger | Bernardsville, NJ |
| regular special | Janice Bornstein | Philadelphia, PA |

**Near miss**

Also, Steve Smith of Brooklyn (New York) reports the New York City corrections commissioner, in describing incidents involving violence at the Rikers Island prison, said, "We will arrest any inmate who misbehaves." Sounds like sorta cruel and usual punishment to me.

**We will arrest any
inmate who misbehaves**

### Thanks for the Vague Memory

Now then, to all who tried (albeit in vane, or, for you purists, vein) to get even, I thank you—although you have risen to new heights of disrespect. Incidentally, you'll be pleased to learn that as a function of your contributions, we (read: I) are now in a financial position to add a new wing to the (former) Oxymoron Institute of North America (and Georgia)—and also a second floor to go with the third floor. Next year we hope to add the first floor. (Think skyhook.) Bottoms up!

Did I mention the form on page 95? Then what are you waiting for? This may be your last chance until next time. Act now (dance later).

Televised hearings

# 3 Oxymorons in the News: Old News & Modern History

Now that I am addicted to oxymorons (did I mention that?), it is a little more than impossible for me *not* to find them everywhere—just as it now is, has been, and will continue to be for you (but only for life; hang on, it's almost over). Further, being justifiably paranoid, I'm not sure if the media put them out just for me—or if the media just put out.

With this semifirmly in mind, let me give you some examples of oxymorons turning up in somewhat recent current events. Mixed candor compels me to admit reluctantly one reason I want to do this is that my accountant (you remember my personable accountant, who makes house calls) tells me it permits me to take the cost of my television set (the water-cooled steam-operated one), as well as my newspaper and magazine subscriptions, as a business deduction. IRS, are you listening? The operative oxymoron is tax return.

I really suppose if I had a favorite oxymoron between the publication of the original *Jumbo Shrimp* and the first deadline for the current product, they would involve the (a) Sakharov case, (2) *Voyager* flight, and (iii) Iran-contra hearings. Read and/or press on.

*(a) Sakharov case.* Finally, the Russians have done something for us—or at least for me. Consider the now not-so-recent Sakharov case. For the longest time, Andrey Sakharov's status had been that of internal exile (internal exile!). Da, da, a thousand times, da. (Not to be confused with Dada.) It has been suggested by some that he is now a free prisoner.

*(2)* Voyager *flight.* My second other favorite occurred when the airship *Voyager* returned after its dramatic flight around the world. The senior pilot, Dick Rutan, on more than one occasion, described the accomplishment as one of aviation's last firsts. While I would agree that the last first is to be preferred to the first last—or as Churchill suggested "the beginning of the end" . . .

*(iii) Iran-contra hearings.* Finally again, I really suppose my third other favorite current-events oxymoron since we last spoke was, and continues to be (it won't go away), associated with the Iran-contra hearings—a veritable verbal cesspool of oxymorons. My semantic sinuses were semi-completely cleared by the use of the term "limited immunity." And then it got better! (The oxymorons, not the sinuses.)

As a matter of fact, the Iran-contra hearings (whether you were pro-contra or contra-contra) were an incredible source of oxymorons (believe me!); and in the material to follow, I probably intend to re-create all (or more, unless we run out of pages) of those pleasant memories of the summer of '87.

### Limited Immunity, Pro-Contra, Lethal Aid, & Other Almost Perfect Oxymorons from the Iran-Contra Hearings

In case you were out of the room and missed it, there was something called the Iran-contra hearings. It appeared in all the media—as well as on radio and television, *and* in print. Oxymoronically, it was monumental; and it also may have been important for the country—this country. As a matter of fact, at one point Sam Donaldson described it as another mini-firestorm.

Once again, demonstrating civic responsibility, in an attempt to be an informed citizen, I spent a lot of time in front of the television set. (It's better that way—and a lot easier to see the screen.) And no, in answer to your next question, this is not our old air-cooled steam-operated gray-and-gray television set. This was our new one—the white-and-white one powered by the brace of gerbils.

In any event, try as I might (and I am and/or do), I was unable *not* to perceive the oxymorons. Therefore, return with us now to those thrilling days of yesteryear when out of the past came the thundering hoofbeats of such oxymorons as Lieutenant Colonel Oliver North's being described as a villainous hero. We also heard about second initiatives and subsequent initiatives. And unless I misunderstood, Secretary of State George Shultz said something about giving lie detector tests on a regular random basis. (Timing is everything, almost, usually.) He also gave us passive reply.

We also heard one-sided dialogue and interactive soliloquy. (Had only Hamlet, Jack Benny, and/or Mel Brooks known.) Also consider somewhat informed, working dinner, and partly engaged. And no one (but me . . . and maybe you) even sadly smirked when military intelligence raised its head again, and again. But how about the rest of the genre—military thought, military etiquette, military salvation, and/or military propriety? Talk about about-face saving!

Others turning up at the appropriately wrong time were certain risk, vociferous silence, Reagan credibility, public secrecy, simple system, legal thought, and (you pick it) weak president and strong president. Did I hear certain doubt? Sure, maybe.

When not blowing smoke, my fellow Hoosier, Admiral John Poindexter, talked about vague recollection, as well as pure nonsense. Arthur Lyman gave us great detail, in great detail. (I must get the name of his barber.) Someone said something about something being somewhat incompatible (I'm not even sure that fits here).

Dan Rather produced the evergreen "What did the president know, and when did he forget it?" (I'm surprised Dan Rather never rubs anyone wrong. It's simply amazing.)

While I can't give credit and/or blame (I'm not licensed in this state), on one day of the hearings we got extensive briefing, somewhat extraordinary, practical theory, censorship freedom, negative concurrence (agreed?), closed hearing, general specificity, exact nebulousness (right on! almost), cabinet government, narrow breadth—as well as the now new classic, lost finding (find and ye shall seek). My somewhat erased notes also suggest some would (and sorta did) argue—and offer compelling evidence—that political embarrassment is an oxymoron.

I think I also heard natural artifact, graphic language, narrow leeway, and poor intelligence—but what do I know? (And when will I know it?)

Someone(s) (not me!) contributed rather honorable, essentially honorable, somewhat tawdry (awright!), simple conspiracy (simple conspiracy!), patriotic conspiracy, and legal conspiracy. And did I hear the statistician's delight, 100%+? (I mean, give it all you've got, plus!)

And how did you feel about congressional cooperation? CIA cooperation? Slight surprise, almost surprised, and/or somewhat legal? I suppose it's all a question of need satisfaction. But whose? (Albert Maslow, where are you when we need you?)

We were also treated to (or subjected to, if you prefer) questioned answer, explicit innuendo (very close enough!), indirect communication, and somewhat unusual (which in itself . . . ).

These attempts to communicate (Pollyanna lives! but not well) notwithstanding, one of my favorites was direct circumvention (it's hard to get around that one)—although you may prefer known covert operation. I've yet to make up my mind about working staff. Also try forced option, one option, disloyal patriot, subjective data, congressional cutoff (sounds more like required elective minor surgery to me), complete testimony, CIA record (I think we have the album on $33\frac{1}{4}$), and real contradiction. Representative Dante Fascell offered normal politics (boggle, boggle), although he later weakly countered with legitimate politics (terminal boggle).

With increasing pessimism, all searched for the original truth, although Robert McFarlane (among others, or, for you purists, *inter alia*) was aversively fond of saying, "I don't recall being aware . . ." A modest oxymoron indeed compared to almost certain, almost certainly.

To elaborate briefly, I am blithely concerned about armed pacifists engaging in positive resistance—a condition absolutely probably leading to increasing depression, rising deficits, but not lower inflation.

Peter Jennings politely zinged us when he talked about the possibility that Lieutenant Colonel

North would do his presentation "slightly out of view." Somehow, I can't quite see that—and I peeked! (But perhaps too soon.)

Consider blameless villains, culprits, criminals, lawyers, thieves, and/or terrorists. Consider them, but please don't elect and/or appoint them.

Oh yes, Sam Donaldson gave us "a little ironic." Isn't that strange and unexpected? If we were into pleonasms yet (and you soon will be, trust me), I would suggest an odd irony; but . . .

Some would argue house counsel is an oxymoron—although I suspect few would argue about disinformation, no information, and/or unclear information. Okay, so argue, some.

And I feel somewhat confident that Representative James Courter, in response to Peter Jennings, said, "I'm sure I didn't understand your question." Finally, something to hold onto! (Or, for you purists, something onto which to hold.) (Onto.)

In terms of rank oxymorons (pun intended, but not the one you're thinking of, or, for you purists, the one of which you are thinking), we were treated to Lieutenant Colonel, Sergeant Major, Major General, Vice Admiral, Rear Admiral, First Lieutenant, Second Lieutenant, and First Class Private. I don't recall Petty Officer, which is just as well because I'm not sure if that's an oxymoron or the opposite of an opposite (which is . . .)—but we did hear more than we cared to about junior officers.

I don't know about you (but I do care, superficially), but I was a little concerned when one witness was described (accurately!) as being a shredding expert. I mean, I prefer cheese as much as the next beefeater (as a matter of fact, I think I'll have the next Beefeater now, please), but that one really tears me up; although I'd be willing to give it a rip (ouch!).

Mr. McFarlane gave us generally aware, while Senator Warren Rudman gave us rather direct (hey, ask Vice President Bush!—he thinks that's a pleonasm! I'm getting to it; I'm getting to it!).

Not to be outdone, Senator Sam Nunn gave us diminished confidence (I feel better already).

Senator Rudman's relatively obscure wasn't shucks (with apologies to Twain's mark) compared to bicameral unity. I'm also in partial awe of guilty scapegoats, self-dependent (don't think about it, it will only confuse me), and exact estimate (at least as near as I can figure it).

I'm not completely unsure the following occurred; but, therefore notwithstanding, I can handle them with clumsy sophistication (or, as we say in Atlanta, clumsy sophistication): broad compartmentalization, exposed insulation, four-cornered triangle, coarse diplomat, and apparently civil government. And I'm absolutely unclear about committee work, CIA management, uniform scraps (double gasp!), straightforward subterfuge, foreign policy continuity, military accountability, and bipartisan cooperation.

Did I hear Lieutenant Colonel North say something about faculty understanding? Obedient defiance I can understand, but what about long recess, legitimate conspiracy, absent witness, totalitarian democracy, conscripted volunteer (is it too late for me to freeze my draft card?), and unique uniform? I stand down (at least semantically).

I also think we came to loose gridlock (as contrasted with tight flexibility) when we got fairly comprehensive. Although, truth be told (and wouldn't that be refreshing?), Senator William Cohen delighted me with somewhat disturbing (not to be outdone by Representative Henry Hyde when he gave us half-true, a little deceptive, and ambiguous law. Exactly!) And did you notice Robert Owen was described as a conservative activist (you think that's easy?)?

If we were into pleonasms yet (and I appreciate we're not, perhaps even more than do you), I would report that someone gave us "prepare to commence." Hey, let us begin, initially.

You may also recall (albeit forgetfully) there was a southern front, an Atlantic front, and . . . an internal front (internal front?).

I also think I heard a positive calamity—unless that was a false fact. Who was it whom said the question, "Which first version?"—oh, *that* first version!

I suppose the preliminary conclusion to almost all of this would be that this was a highly visible covert operation. But somehow I just can't see it. (I may be the only one.) Although I'm sure it was "fairly obvious" to Representative Hyde. But you have to remember it was he, Hyde, who talked about responsible oversight. Wow! But I'm willing to overlook it if he is—although he also did talk about half-democracies. To be somewhat fair, he didn't say *which* half.

Representative Courter yet (and yet) once again was also "somewhat confused." At this point take a number. Mr. McFarlane may have won some sort of minor oxymoron prize with his comment "somewhat fairly explicit." (Gasp! or even more.) But then, he also described Lieutenant Colonel North as essentially a cynical humanitarian. (C'mon, you think *that's* easy? You really have to not like liking people you like to pull that off well.)

You tell me, who was the interviewer on C-SPAN who asked the *Washington Post* representative, "Do we expect any surprises?" Had he asked me that question, I almost certainly would have responded with the questionable answer "Almost always." (Maybe that's why no one ever asks me anything. Just ask me.)

"It's very important that I do not know." Hey, don't you know it?

Tom Brokaw reported someone (I forget who, because I fell asleep) spoke with what could be described only as a dynamic monotone. This is pillow talk? Whoopie!

You may also remember Donald Regan was extremely neutral through all this, although I think someone did suggest he went through an unusual routine.

And I think it was Attorney General Edwin Meese who talked about normal espionage. (Think about it, it will sneak up on you.) It was not I (or even me) who suggested Meese investigation was/is an oxymoron, the consistent discrepancies notwithstanding.

I'm still chewing on contra aid, contra assistance, and pro-contra. I'm somewhat certain I'm either for it or against it. Independent counsel? Perhaps certainly.

To some (include I, me, or, for you purists, us), Admiral Poindexter's six-million-dollar detail qualifies as an oxymoron. As a matter of fact, that's more money than I received as the advance on this book. No, seriously; I mean it. If you don't believe me, ask my giving creditors.

As far as independent counsel, legal brief clearly was the order of the day. But also consider simple technology, initial resignation, initial retirement, active reserve, minor issue, normal controversy, real hypothetical, and CIA requests (oh, please!).

Also, were you impressed (then-Captain) Poindexter had been described as a thorough briefer. You have to be very fast, a lot.

Representative Michael DeWine thought something was a little misleading. Maybe, but I must have been looking the wrong way; I missed it. Possibly that was the public covert policy, or whatever had nearly succeeded, or the intelligence oversight board. Did two different chains of command get your attention? Until now? Who's in charge here, in charge here?

And have you considered Sandinista compliance? Contra aid? Opponents of contra aid? Anti-contra? (Wow! Hey, wait; that's a palindrome! [Wow, not anti-contra; anti-contra is a pleonasm, I think.]) Contra threat?

Two of my favorites were Senator Nunn's dissemble. That's putting it all together, sort of.

But it was Admiral Poindexter who talked about a low-profile public approach, which I suppose is conventional wisdom. And while Republican hopeful (I didn't say it) Governor Pete du Pont did describe moderate Iranians as an oxymoron during a debate at Dartmouth, it was Representative Hyde who laid that one on us earlier during the televised hearings. (Senator Biden, where are you now that we need you?)

Who talked about the whole hemisphere? (I mean, no half ways here.) Possibly the same person who gave us partial conclusion or pure speculation. I'm still mulling over Representative Hyde's "almost a negative pregnancy." (I suppose it's conceivable.) Anyway, I'm glad the hearings were televised, because televised hearings . . .

In conclusion, for now, it has been suggested the entire Iran-contra hearings could be summarized by suggesting, that, to some, the Boland Amendment was an oxymoron.

Ha! And you thought oxymorons had absolutely no socially redeeming quality . . . and maybe you were right. Big deal!

## *Time* Magazine: Oxymoronic Hog Heaven

Among the many personal faults—and even shortcomings—about which I boast, neatness is not included; or at least if it were, I seem to have misplaced it. Therefore, before my spouse (do you suppose the plural of *spouse* really is *spice?*) disposes of the *Time* magazines neatly piled in my randomly organized library, let me re-create (did you see the oxymoron? Stay alert!) the point about oxymorons being where you find them—and among the several places you can find them most easily are *Time* magazine, and *M\*A\*S\*H* (but we'll save *M\*A\*S\*H* for another day . . . or at least another chapter).

I previously indicated how office space and closet space were particularly poignant personal oxymorons per myself. (Phew!) In any event, in my usual unprecedented fit of domestic cooperation (read: I had no choice), I recently resentfully agreed to have my long-standing, long-suffering roommate (*must* she refer to our marriage as the Thirty Years' War?) dump the larger half of my declining collection (a collection giveaway?) of *Time*s.

Certainly perhaps not unlike you, I hate to give anything up. After all, you might need something someday—such as that pith helmet, the 1949 calendar (almost new), the only slightly used dental floss, and other even less obvious things. In any event, systematically at random, as I pluck the throwaways from the good garbage, following is some (prime) *Time* stuff:

11 JAN 88: The article on the Teflon Twins of 1988 yielded television tape, former evangelist (I believe), minor peccadillo, boastful exaggerations (I know it's *not* an oxymoron; it's a pleonasm; and I'm getting to it; I just wanted to see if you were paying attention), and "as other candidates pepper their rivals with grapeshot." And how about preacher politicians, perfectly legitimate (pleonasm, gotcha again), safe politics, respective conventions, and tenuous ties.

In an article on pushy New York (some would argue . . .) panhandlers appear belligerent begging, antipoverty workers, aggressive begging, little hope, and noticeably less aggressive. Brother, can you spare an oxymoron?

28 DEC 87: This issue contains an ad for Federal Express. An article on Gary Hart contained purely political. Additional oxymorons in that article include high negative, "unfavorable ratings that are higher than," and Democratic Party. Also appearing (but without selected short subjects) was: "If this weren't so serious, it would be funny. If it weren't so funny, it would be serious." That turned me all the way halfway around. Also, political process and the delightfully oxymoronic reinvent. Think about it. So what's new?

I was also casually concerned about "front-page *Des Moines Register.*"

A January 1988 issue of *Time* described Jimmy Breslin as being "happiest when he is making himself (and others) angry." Way to go, Jimmy! Enjoy, enjoy! . . . if you can.

In the Food section, the chutzpah award was given to someone who brought her New York Texas cheesecake to, of all places, New York (New York). Maybe certainly, but I prefer mine barbecued, hold the slaw—that's how they do it in North Carolina, with slaw—in both hands, please.

Show Business section: The Goldwynism "I read part of it all the way through" is included along with a description of Orson Welles's always seeking perfection, or better. Persevere. Missed it by that much!

And speaking of Orson Welles and barbecue, there is a barbecue restaurant here in Atlanta whose sign out front shyly proclaimed: "We will serve no swine before its time." It's time; they're here. (The sign currently speaks, somewhat eloquently, of serious barbecue.)

The Cinema section talked about John Huston being wonderfully ambiguous, and suggested *Broadcast News* was wickedly nice.

Moving right along, a November 1987 issue quoted Senator Paul Simon (remember him?) saying he "went away from Easter Service in downtown Stuttgart very much uninspired." There's a lot of that going around . . . and around.

IBM (which is neither a missile nor a necessary bodily function) had an ad entitled "Small News from IBM."

An interesting piece of writing in the Sexes section: "has engaged several married couples." Timing is still everything.

2 NOV 87: This issue describes General Secretary Mikhail Gorbachev as a devout atheist. No comment, and you can quote me on that.

The Letters section featured "Soviet life" and "home offices." Two writes do not make a wrong. An oxymoronic contribution, yes.

The same issue also asks the penetrating question "Can cohabiting ruin marriage?" How soon do you need an answer? (But almost seriously, don't you hate people who answer a question with a question? But on the other hand, what's wrong with that?) Also another article about Ivan Boesky, although I note they still do not mention this year's awarding of the Ivan Boesky Ethics Prize. Competition is keen, if not honest.

24 AUG 87: ". . . is in an advanced state of decline" appears. Eastern Airlines turns up, as does persistent ambivalence. I give in; I guess not; no . . . Hang in there, for sure I guess.

How about inferred petty corruption, or discreet corruption? I'll never tell, more than once.

9 MAR 87: The Books section includes wickedly funny, hilarious funerals, jocular murder trials, and droll executions. Not tonight, dear, I have a headache. Couldn't we just go to an O-rated movie? (such as *Ironweed* or *Rebel Without a Cause* or *A Fine Mess* or *Endless Summer* or *Wrong Is Right* or *Not Quite Paradise* or . . . )

5 OCT 87: A subtitle to the Biden writing affair reads: "Another Democrat Self-Destructs with Help from His Rivals." Okay, but frankly, I'm against rivals; but with rivals like that, who needs friendly enemies?

28 SEP 87: Smokeless cigarette. Does that mean we'll have smokeless and nonsmokeless sections on airplanes with scheduled flight times of less than two minutes? It makes sense to me . . . and that's one less reason why I'm not worried.

Somewhere else in the same issue it was reported some prisoners were discovered missing. That's not easy—even in our undercrowded criminal justice system. In an article on the Reverend Pat Robertson (remember him?) appeared verbal italics (I *like* it!) and high negative ratings (Gary Hart, roll over!). The latter no doubt was a clerical error—not to be confused with clerical heir. (Okay, have it your way . . . to be confused with clerical heir.)

29 FEB 88: An article entitled "Please Turn Off the Dog" begins: "Now that you've had your frozen diet gourmet TV dinner . . ." A five-part, if not five-star, oxymoron.

23 NOV 87: A delightful letter-to-the-editor regarding the controversy associated with *The Random House Dictionary of the English Language: Second Edition Unabridged* (I somewhat hope they got the pronunciation of "oxymoron" correct this time), in which the reader writer wrote, "In other words, ain't is okay, but everyone are ain't." Aren't it the truth! (he said candidly).

Another reader in responding to that settled controversy talked about a somewhat narrow attitude. Okay; after all, the way I see it, everyone is entitled to my opinion.

25 MAY 87: The late Rita Hayworth was described as the all-American love goddess. Sigh, *sí!* (With insincere apologies to Mel Blanc.)

The issue also pointed up Woody Allen's fight against computerized coloring of classic films. I share his happy anguish; and I trust he will be anxiously pleased to learn there is little or no truth to the secret rumor that will soon be circulating that he and I and a fourth person are in the process of developing a procedure whereby color films will be computerized into black-and-white. (And I certainly hope that won't be taken as an off-color remark; after all, this is a child's book. I know, I wrote it myself.)

And as my first last *Time* sinks slowly in the outgoing good garbage, we say *aloha, adieu, adiós,* and *Willkommen* to that bare treasure trove, as well as my now *Time*less library.

**Working dinner**

**Just a Few More Random and/or Miscellaneous (but Not Other) Oxymorons from the Media**

In addition, because I didn't know what to do with the balance of my notes (please, no hints! Besides, I think that's anatomically impossible—or at least highly improbable), following are a few random and/or miscellaneous (but not other) oxymorons from the media. Incidentally, I am informed the term "happy medium" is—or is not—descriptive of Jeane Dixon after a successfully unsuccessful prophetic prophecy, even when it's a pleonasm (oops, not yet; forget you saw that—yeah, sure, just try).

NBC News' Ken Bode on (roughly) September 11, 1987, suggested the possibility that Gary Hart had a high negative image. (Which I suppose is only slightly less better than having a low positive image.)

Meanwhile, back in Atlanta (my current hometown), a local anchorman said something along the lines of "[Their life is] often unpredictable." Ah, if only I could pretty much count on that.

And how many times have you heard the delightful oxymoron "silken bonds"? . . . or slipped them (if you're into, whoops, out of, that sort of thing).

And finally, as I think I may have indicated elsewhere, here in Atlanta, weather forecast remains a cruel oxymoron. Each year, as opposed to first annual, we get caught by surprise by the snowfall—*any* snowfall. As a matter of fact again, one of my favorite oxymorons remains the City of Atlanta Snow Removal Plan. But I wouldn't want you to think we're not prepared, not on the ball. We are. We get both trucks out—right away. As a former erudite midwesterner, I find it commonly curious to find people putting down pepper, inasmuch as we have no salt . . . and even less experience.

End of press release; press on.

# 4  My Ten Favorite Oxymorons: But Who Counts?

Two of the most frequent, penetrating, and incisive questions I am often occasionally asked are "Where is the washroom?" and "What are your favorite oxymorons?" . . . although not necessarily in that order. Ordinarily, I cleverly sidestep both questions by coyly responding, "None of your business" or, "Who wants to know?" Or, if I am particularly glib that particular day, I really nail the truth-seeker with "Oh, yeah?" However, I think the time has come to respond—at least to the second question. (It is too late for the first. Uncanny.)

Of course, in all partial truth, asking me what my ten favorite oxymorons are is not unlike asking a parent who their favorite child is. It is grossly unfair (and I can't wait to respond). The gross unfairness notwithstanding, following, in random order (alphabetically according to height), are my ten all-time temporary favorite oxymorons, today.

| | | |
|---|---|---|
| jumbo shrimp | military intelligence | academic salary |
| intense apathy | standard deviation | civil war |
| student athlete | negative momentum | real magic |
| mobile home | loyal opposition | perfect misfit |
| first annual | downtown Detroit | extremely bland |
| gregarious recluse | slightly pregnant | social psychologist |
| pro-contra | firm maybe | plastic glasses |
| limited immunity | same difference | educational television |
| man child | almost suddenly | uptown Buffalo |
| business ethics | somewhat awesome | extremely average |

| | | |
|---|---|---|
| down escalator | academic dean | civil engineer |
| systematic variance | objective rating | criminal justice |
| completely educated | legal brief | barely dressed |
| postal service | planned serendipity | whole hemisphere |
| student teacher | random order | press release |
| beyond infinity | guest host | nondairy creamer |
| internal exile | Columbia football | perhaps predictably |
| Amtrak schedule | greater Cleveland | $N + 1$ |

But who counts? (besides laid-back compulsives?)

# 5

## After-Dinner Speaking, & Other Sources of Oxymorons & Dyspepsia

One of the other more or less pleasant benefits or penalties (I haven't decided yet which, but almost certainly not neither) associated with this extremely meaningful nonsense has been after-dinner speaking (I wonder if I could get anyone interested in some before-dinner speaking) and the frequently intense disinterest by the media—particularly radio.

As I indicated last time, interesting speech and talk show are among my top $10 \pm 20$ favorite oxymorons. With predictable irony, I was able to contribute mightily to my own happy demise.

It was an appropriate happenstance that the name of one organization to which I was invited to speak (or, for you purists, which I was invited to speak to) was an oxymoronic find—although not a single oxymoron came from the interaction. The name of that organization? Parents Without Partners! (Wow! The hard way! Don't think about it.) And while I understand the good, and unfortunately necessary, work this single-parent support group does, you have to admit it must be some sort of unwritten record for biological oxymorons. (Although I do allow I did cut class the day we covered that particular topic in high school. You don't suppose . . . Naw!)

Following are just a few (I insincerely promise) more organizations, along with their oxymoronic fallout. While I cannot give individual credit (or is it discredit?), you know who you are . . . and I'll never forgive you. Thanks. Forget it—and remember that!

### Artificial Intelligence, Mega Bits, & Other Almost Perfect High-Tech Oxymorons

Just prior to Easter weekend 1987, I presented the keynote address to the Rocky Mountain Information Processing and Communication Exhibition and Conference (Data Marketing Association) in Denver. While the small crowd was indifferently attentive, the oxymoron contest we ran was somewhat functional. In retrospect, I suspect the strength of the contest may have been the prize structure. First prize was one copy of *Jumbo Shrimp*, second prize was two copies of *Jumbo Shrimp*, and . . .

Anyway, here are some of the entries (many of which did indeed have something to do with high technology) generated by this particular group: free society, ancient technology, virtual storage, data administration, structure design, dry runs (you said it; not me!), random file organization, expert consultant, dip switch (well, I'll be switched!), data processing, micro-mainframe, half-word (I guess if you talk fast enough . . .), logical design, sophisticated hacker, hard-wired, data structure, expert business system, chilling fever, and infinite loop (think about it, about it, about it . . .).

**Ancient technology**

However, my personal favorites from the contributions were user-friendly and personal computer. At the risk of sounding like Andy Rooney, have you ever wondered if personal computer is a true oxymoron or a quasi oxymoron?

Incidentally, the two winning oxymorons were large-scale mini-computers and lady mud wrestler. You may be wondering what lady mud wrestler has to do with high technology—and you may continue to do so. It was never clear (as in mud) to me either; but we all had a swell evening together.

But when I woke the next morning, the hotel in which I was staying was being picketed. (*I* thought I had made a better presentation than that!) It turned out the American Atheists convention was meeting in the same hotel; and the picketers were religious fundamentalists. It was a very interesting few days before I returned to Atlanta; and I was particularly impressed with the liberal fundamentalists and the pious atheists. A good time was had by all—although it could hardly be described as a passive confrontation. Welcome home, stranger.

### Mensa of Georgia Meets the Oxymoron: A Case of Mutual Overmatch

I addressed Mensa of Georgia (no, I don't think so). As an academic scholar (hey, that's one of those P words; what's *that* doing here?), I was anxious not to make a fool of myself. The evening went well.

But before I forget, some of the more memorable oxymorons contributed were high-level depression, black light, flaccid erection, rational ravings (almost no comment), real fantasy, shyly pompous (as in the last days of), dry well, congressional responsibility, morbid humor, balanced insanity, hot ice, small crowd (push came to shove), leisure suit, half dead (ah, but *which* half?), honest convict, Plymouth Reliant (how do you like that one, Lee? Would you believe Dodge

Ram?), demanding patient, personalized form letter, anxious patient, convinced skeptic (well, maybe), mutual aversion, deliberate mistake, and pronounced silence (just so long as it's not mispronounced).

My personal favorite was the Second Annual Tour of Classic New Homes—although I must confess honest convict and leisure suit got my attention.

Someone did suggest "Solipsists of the World, Unite." Okay, but one at a time, please . . . and stay in line.

Good stuff? You bet; but you have to remember this was the meeting at which was asked the philosophically sticky question "What makes the Teflon stick to the pan?" My educated guess is nonstick Velcro.


## Closet Space, Uncomplicated Move, Permanent Lease, & Other Almost Perfect Apartment Owner and Manager Oxymorons

Another after-dinner opportunity I had was in Atlanta with the Apartment Owners and Managers Association. The 400+ individuals who showed up enjoyed themselves; we'll never know about the approximately 05,003 no-shows. (Incidentally, your dinner is getting warm.)

In addition to the oxymorons I was able to contribute (for example, waste management, routine emergency, rising deficits, Braves highlight [and lucky to have that, at that], Falcon football, full-time hobby, resident manager, uptown Duluth [local joke], shared monopoly), those who *were* there presented me with polite Yankee, mobile home, satisfied tenant, partially furnished, downtown Snellville (local joke counterpoint), peace offensive (I *don't know* why), apartment home, City of Atlanta Snow Removal Plan (I *told* you!), natural synthetic, free love, original copy, and negative income.

**47**

However, somehow I sensed I had not quite made my point when, after the meeting, someone came up with killed dead (dare I tell him that's one of those other things? Y'know, the P word).

## The Fairly Great Atlanta NBC Affiliate Oxymoron Safari

One of the more interesting TV experiences I had was with a local Atlanta NBC affiliate. A promising media personality, who still has not provided me with the promised videotape of our project, asked if we could go on an oxymoron hunt in a local shopping mall. And, while I understand the lengthy edited snippet was nominated for a local Emmy, I believe the real positive gain (did you see the pleonasm? Pay attention and/or be alert!) came from the oxymorons discovered on that nonromantic semantic safari.

**Nondairy creamer**

Passively armed with only my (then) trusted television personality, camera person, clip board, ink pencil, fearless intrepidation, and that pith helmet I told you about on page 35 (that I *knew* I would need someday), and feeling for all the world like Stewart Granger on a good day, or Robert Redford on a bad day, I stalked the ubiquitous—but frequently occurring—oxymoron. We climbed down up escalators and scaled up down staircases—or was it the other way around? A good time was had by all; and there was a worthwhile haul. As almost a matter of fact, several of the oxymorons have been stuffed and hung on my library wall; the other ends extend into our bedroom. A biased random sample of the clean kill follows.

In a gourmet shop, we bagged low-cal sweetener, weight watcher's pizza, onion pickles, liquid smoke, mild taco salsa, and frozen food. Old friends from *Jumbo Shrimp* also appeared. Remember turkey ham? Ham bologna? Nondairy creamer? Sweet-and-sour sauce? White chocolate? Plain caviar? Instant espresso? They all send regards, incidentally—and ask why you never write (you could at least call). And, my most recent all-time favorite food oxymoron, fresh raisins—remember, you heard it on the grapevine—turned up in the net.

Also, per my wife's demanding request, while there I picked up a five-pack of quick-frozen heat-and-serve ice (conventional microwave). We weren't expecting any guests; and they're heavy drinkers—he weighs about 250 and she has been known to drink heavies to excess.

Incidentally, this was the local TV station that had tried to change its image by describing itself as a "New Tradition," but not quite yet. Also, the shopping center to which we went was neither Perimeter Center East nor Perimeter Center West, although we were unluckily fortunate enough to find a parking space. We noticed grazing designer sweatshirts.

In the restaurant area, we discovered what you might expect, albeit serendipitously. Cheesecake, designer water, jumbo shrimp (jumbo shrimp! Be still, my heart), crab cakes, fast food. However, my personal favorite was strawberry lemonade (they just don't grow them the way they used to). That's reminiscent of fried roast beef, which is rarely well-done.

In a search of clothing stores, we found virgin wool (who cares about their morals? Tom said sheepishly), real synthetic, affordable furs, dress jeans, designer jeans, Western style, real polyester, Texas chic. Sound all too familiar? It occurred to me that all of these things contribute to an air of casual formality.

At one of the sneaker shops, we ran fun run to earth, as well as dress sneaker, self-service, and the lowest high point of the day, speed walking.

In one of the bookstores, we sighted *Limited Power, Almost Paradise, Close Relations, Dirty White, Darkness at Noon, The Agony and the Ecstasy,* and *A Perfect Spy. Jumbo Shrimp* was difficult to find.

Realizing again oxymorons did indeed abound, we pushed on to a video/music store, where we found *Bad Medicine, Deadly Blessing, Pee Wee's Big Adventure, Blade Runner, Urban Cowboy, Fail-Safe, Perfect Strangers,* and other old friends such as Boy George, rock music, "The Lady Is a Tramp," "Alone Together," Quiet Riot, The Fifth Dimension, *Down and Out in Beverly Hills, Back to the Future, Garbo Talks,* and *Mr. Mom* (as in Hi). All in all, it was an excitingly uneventful day (and not unlike Atlanta, a nice place to live but I wouldn't want to visit there).

And while I still wait here at base camp for the oft-promised videotape, feeling very much not unlike Montgomery Clift in *The Heiress,* I do remain fairly sincerely grateful to the individual for the semisound judgment to let my oxymoronic paranoia run mall-amok.

Most of all, though, I was pleased to have validated my common sense in retaining that pith helmet all these years. Did I mention I have a slight lisp?

And then, almost suddenly it happened, and happened again, and continued to happen again . . . and again. Repeatedly, perhaps even redundantly, if you will (and even if you won't), in the course of the radio call-in open-line interviews, a frequently, but as it turns out, erroneously, submitted oxymoron was free gift—as well as cash money, hot water heater, killed dead . . .

Generally, at this point, a lot of hemming and hawing took place between and/or among the host, me (I myself personally am an excellent hemmer, but only a fair hawer), and the somewhat confused, but imminently cutoffable, caller-inner. Fortunately, I was usually saved by an electric power failure, but not often enough. Frequently often I was cornered. I knew these erroneously submitted phrases were *not* oxymorons (because that was *all* I knew); but *what* were they?

### The P Word: Have the Young Children Leave the Room

Awful terrible horror of awful terrible horrors, the Robert Frost quotation I have in my office had returned back to haunt me—and it was (and still is): "There are a lot of completely educated people in this world, and of course they would resent to learn anything new." As we say in bullfighting and teaching (and yes, there is an extremely fine small slight subtle difference—having to do with the distribution system), this was crunch time, a moment of truth. I myself *had* to learn something new! Frost was right, I did—and do—resent that, deeply.

In any event, what happened was, I had to learn what pleonasms were. And so long as *I* had to learn, *you* are going to have to learn. Don't worry, they're only slightly more addictive than oxymorons (too late, gotcha, yet again!).

This part of the book is preoccupied in depth with pleonasms. Pleonasms are not unlike oxymorons: I'm never sure whether I need to defend them or define them. (But unlike oxymorons, frankly, I don't give a care, Scarlett.) Once again, it's rather like playing trivia (albeit this time unimportant trivia). Either you know it or you don't—and from now on, you know it, don't you know it?

Therefore, in an attempt to stay alertly awake (me, not you) and fully consciously aware of the possibility of insulting at least one group of readers (let alone the nonreading illiterates)—although I'm not sure which, the exact half that does know about pleonasms, or the equal half that does not—let me again initially begin with pronunciation and definition. (Yes, *Jumbo Shrimp* readers, you're right. As I seem to remember Yogi Berra say, "It's déjà vu all over again." [Did you catch that one?])

**Cash money**

Old professors, and habits, die hard—two conditions for which I am somewhat grateful—the students' position regarding the former condition notwithstanding.

## Pronunciation

"Pleonasm" is only slightly hardly more difficult to pronounce than "oxymoron"—and you know my history on that one. The best sound advice I can give you is, don't mispronounce it incorrectly. Street people in public places will laugh at you if you do. Rather, better pronounce it exactly the same way it sounds and looks. (We'll work on the spelling later . . . or after that.)

## Definition

Contrary to what you might be thinking, "pleonasm" is not an uncomfortable clumsy awkward term that comes up when you and your maturing child gropingly reach toward puberty—his or hers, not yours—and have *that* discussion about sex education. (As a matter of fact, sex education just may be . . . ) But rather, pleonasms are just the opposite of oxymorons. Would you believe the opposite of opposites? How about contradiction contradictions? Would you settle for semantic verbal overkill?

A pleonasm is two concepts (usually two words) that are redundant. Let me say that again, a pleonasm is two concepts (usually two words) that are redundant. I mean, how many times do I have to say it? It is the bringing together of redundant expressions. Consider free gift, frozen ice, sharp point, widow woman, microdot, dark night, exact same, real actual, light white, cold frost, small speck, academic scholarship, dark black, hot fire, classic tradition, killed dead.

Unlike oxymorons (ha!), pleonasms are an addictive (remember, you auditorily heard it here) semantic phenomenon that no one, with the possible exception of you, me (or, for you semipurists, I), and literate English teachers cares about—beginning just exactly right now. They (pleonasms, not literate English teachers) have been described by some as the dark side of oxymorons. Faint, but damning, positive praise indeed!

### Ubiquitous and Insidious (Sound Familiar So Far?)

Further, planned intentional use and/or unplanned unintentional use of pleonasms apparently appears to be growing greater. What has come to be known as "poor writing" is closely akin to pleonasms. (We were made for each other; it's a match made in word heaven.) They are every English teacher's twenty-four-hour-a-day nightmare. Further, besides being ubiquitous and insidious, they appear to be everywhere . . . and frequently.

Having already verbally told you in words how this particular semantic gaff hooked me, let me make a few nontheoretical empirical observations. My multiple purposes in this part of the initial preliminary first material on pleonasms is to describe the ubiquitous and insidious nature of this minute small unimportant trivial semantic phenomenon (you *do* see where we're going, don't you?); to raise your awareness level about this most recent latest unhealthy semantic sickness of mine; to infect and/or addict you (everything should be so easy); and to continue to again ruin your life, again. Got all that? Good—or more accurately, pleonastically, extremely good! . . . or perhaps even very excellent!

Toward doing this, I've already told you how this gratis free gift cost me dearly. What I would like to do in the subsequent following next chapter is to tell you verbally, show you graphically how these sly little devils bedevil our everyday daily speech and writing. But however, be warned that pleonasms, not unlike oxymorons, are also *not* for everybody—only those who read, write, speak, and/or listen, as well as probably possibly youthful teenagers and/or university college students.

What follows may remind you of every piece of poor bad writing and/or bad poor speaking you've ever had the negative misfortune to which to be exposed (or, for you purists, to which to be exposed to); and thank you.

Incidentally, as was *not* the case with oxymorons, for which I made the discriminating distinction between true and quasi oxymorons, I make no such definitive distinction here. Bad evil is as bad evil does. Although the more I think about it, federal deficit . . .

As with oxymorons (and oxymoron sources), my advice is *not* to go looking for pleonasms. Once again, when I am often frequently asked by rabid zealots, "Dr. Blumenfeld, where can I find the ubiquitous and insidious pleonasm?" my responsive answer, with indulgent patience, is "Relax, pleonasms find you." In point of fact, they may be found in the exact same identical places as oxymorons. How convenient—one-shop stopping.

Therefore ergo, your task, should you choose to accept this assignment, will be only to make a categorical distinction between the cursed two—pleonasms and oxymorons (not The Mummy and Macbeth). It should be an easy task (oops, that's an oxymoron; sorry about that). If you find you cannot make the differential distinction with this narrow definition, my personal individual thoughtfully considered subjective opinion is that you may desire to want to do two things: (a) check your pulse, and (b) dial 911. Repeat that, twice, again.

Okay, prepare to commence—or better yet, get ready. For here we begin to start to go, sliding down the other side of this double-edged razor. You may find that both a sarcastic and a cutting remark, but . . . Remember to recall, pleonasms are redundant redundancies, contradiction contradictions, semantic overkills, repeated redundancies, excessive excessiveness, and, most of all, redundant redundancies.

# 7 Redundant Pleonasms Arranged, Sorted, & Grouped

## PLEONASMS, MISCELLANEOUS: VERY UNIQUE CORRECT SOLUTION

I decided to make up my mind to call this initial first section on pleonasms Miscellaneous for obvious reasons (but of course you knew that). Remember to recall, should you have a problem—or difficulty—distinguishing between what should be in the Miscellaneous section, as opposed to the Other section, as opposed to the Unclassified section, refer to the descriptive definition of pleonasms on page 54. If that fails, check your local yellow pages . . . your real local yellow pages. And verbally speaking of yellow pages, you've surely certainly heard about the professor whose lecture notes were so old, when he dropped them in class, they broke. Boy, was I embarrassed!

But however, totally independent of that, I wouldn't want you to think my marital connubial life is totally complete wedded bliss. Occasionally, my marital spouse and I do have arguments during which time we disagree about things. For example, the other day she falsely accused me of not listening (at least I think that's what she said); and while . . . On the other hand, I am listening now (I said, I am listening now), and following are some verbally said, literally written, and other pleonastic panache that have recently called me to their attention.

Old customs (and nocturnal vampires) die hard. And so, each every time I see a play actor on stage perform delicate surgery, I think it's very extremely important—or maybe even urgently important—to consider whether or not it is a close shave. Or thoughtfully consider this arranged staged scenario:

The other day, at 12:00 P.M. midday noon, as I was walking alone by myself along a sandy beach, an anonymous stranger, possibly a rabid fan, boasted positively about the wet water.

Noticing her dark black short shorts, and not wishing to come to a complete stop, I clumsily blurted, "Real genuine messy garbage obviously clearly is bad waste." (I have a way with words . . . and occasionally with anonymous strangers.) Irregardless, could you visually picture all that? Honest truth?

Pensive thought: Healthy tan—oxymoron or pleonasm? (Stay attentively alert.)

Now, see if you can find the redundant pleonasms in the following list.

good medicine
positive praise
young child
dive down
wet liquid
barren arid dry desert
phony counterfeit
male rooster
young child
mobile transportation
rural farm
rural farm (I told you they were redundant—you can say that again.)
baby lamb
completely full

How did you do? Very extremely excellent!

Attention, college students and/or parents of college students: Can you remember when fourth-year senior was a pleonasm?

And speaking of irrefutable facts, do you suppose the term "criminal lawyer" is an oxymoron or pleonasm?

As mentioned previously before, before I was a provincial southerner I was a provincial midwesterner. As a matter of fact, until I was about thirty-five years old, I thought Cincinnati *was* the East. (I now know it's a few miles more.) Anyway in spite of that, while my retained memories do not contain many synthetic substitutes, I do recall natural grass, hard concrete, rubber tires, and one particular strange freak who arrived with a traveling mobile touring circus. And while he was a huge monster, given to belligerent violence, his first primary negative fault was that he was a narrow-minded bigot. For example, one dark night he committed the mistaken error of sacrificing a female ewe. (Absolutely for sure, there will never be another. . . . ) Perhaps (I offer sheepishly) he may be forgiven, inasmuch as he admittedly said he was caught up in an angry rage. Oversaturated yet?

Hot water heater. (Gotcha!)

And how many times have you heard:

cold ice
sharp point
passive defense
fraternity brother
round circle
empty vacuum
dark black (Right, you have an excellent good memory.)
major masterpiece

lazy bum
footsteps
final conclusion

Call it jealous envy, but whenever someone raises up an open window, I'm tempted to want to jump up—which is preferable to being tempted to want to fall down.

Having completely everything—or totally nothing—to do with the present conversation (big talk!), my totally perfect memory recalls a high school wood shop teacher who used to tell us to use coarse sandpaper. (Admittedly, it was more functional than the other.) Aye, there's the rub, again.

Now that I'm currently a published author, I nervously worry about things like such as which of the following are oxymorons and which are pleonasms. Certainly for sure, I can use some helpful assistance.

**Nocturnal vampires**

safety glass
young sixty
parental guidance
natural gas
sophisticated New Yorker
extended credit
intelligent fight
bad oxymoron
Big Ten basketball
good sex

I don't suppose anybody would consider cow leather to be a new invention (certainly not the cow); but I think we made a positive gain a short time ago in a recent football game when I heard new rookie, loose fumble, and offensive tackle—all pleonasms, as contrasted with the oxymorons kick return, no gain, completed interception, and partial silence. But rather then, still yet once again, these are but verbal words anyway.

Square corner. (Why not? . . . although it is a matter of degrees.)

Not to be a coarse crude boor, but I'm certainly sure you'd preferably like to review various other miscellaneous pleonasms—as opposed to these various miscellaneous other pleonasms. That absolutely exactly being the case, press on—but before you do, give some reflective thought, or better yet, some planned strategy, or even conscious intention—to contributing your very own pleonasms via the mailer on precisely exactly page 95. Incidentally, cash money is always acceptable (and the right color) if not deductible.

## PLEONASMS, OTHER: ARE YOU OLD ENOUGH TO REMEMBER WHEN HETERO-SEXUAL SEX WAS A PLEONASM?

Old age, not unlike fondly remembered nostalgia, ain't what it used to be—especially old nostalgia. For example, it used to be a negative disadvantage to be an elderly octogenarian in your eighties. No more. These days, *Modern Maturity* would have us believe the ultimate end, the right key, the sought-after goal, would appear to be the same exact thing as for anyone else. Acquiescently, I am forcibly compelled to agree. Some, e.g., sociologists who study recurring relationships, now speak of the old elderly and the (forgive me and/or the oxymoron) young elderly.

Anyway, irregardless (I know, but it's my book; and I can do whatever I want . . . so long as my domineering editor says I can), and in spite of these things notwithstanding, and ongoing continuing indifferent apathy, I am now old enough (and getting older in a quick flash) to remember when the following were pleonasms. (How about you?)

equal halves
genuine original
military soldier
white snow
safety insurance
planned parenthood
plain bagel
road car
flat pancake
close family

beef hamburger
sound as a dollar
blue sky (except in my hometown where I lived when I was
growing up, and various other parts of the Rust Belt)
inactive reserve
dairy cream
southern Mississippi
luxury Cadillac
imprisoned criminal
Hershey's chocolate

**Flat pancake**

New Orleans jazz
IBM computer
Chicago politics
Xerox copier
unpaid amateur

Personal computer: What do you think? Pleonasm or oxymoron? Right! (And/or wrong!)

In case you haven't guessed it, I'm an only child. I recently realized I was engaged in pleonastic behavior when I phoned my mother and said, "Hi, Mom, it's Warren." (But it worked; not only did she recognize the name . . . if not me . . . but she accepted the charges.) If nothing else, I am consistently reproducible. And there's a logical reason for that.

Okay, I admit it, fresh raisins and fresh prunes are two of my favorite food oxymorons; but to be equally fair, empirically demonstrating stubborn persistence, I often seek out sour lemons, sweet sugar, and hot chili (hot chili? Hmm . . .). I also accept clean soap, but I refuse unwanted garbage.

Baseball players (who, you will recall, engage in competitive contests) often refer to a high sky (them are the best kind).

Salty anchovy.

Perhaps I am, as has been reputedly reported, a clumsy oaf; but recently I was thinking about natural gas. Oxymoron or pleonasm? Wrong! (And/or right!)

The other day I received a very important-looking package in the mail loudly proclaiming: "From TV's Ed McMahon." I knew it was very (or maybe even terrifically) important because it also said: "Extremely Urgent." I could only assume it was full of pleonasms, or I had won some kind of sweepstakes. Unfortunately, I won; I was hoping for pleonasms.

I heard a repeatable pleonasm the other day. Someone said that he was still in a rut. Stay with it! . . . Would you believe stationary inertia?

I also heard an unrepeatable pleonasm—which I suppose is an oxymoron. (Check your definitions on pages 54 and 10, as well as your wallet, watch, and coat.)

And how many times have you heard:

three-cornered triangle
a woman pregnant with child (Hey, it's your baby, Rosemary.)
together in tandem
a bald man without hair
sorority sister
three-point field goal
category type
fastened shut
rigid stubbornness
male ram
first things first (Hey, wait a second!)
small speck
female hen
dull lecture (Ouch!)
funny comedy
exciting adventure
dull lecture (Now *cut* that out!)
synthetic substitute

Tony Kubek threw baseball more than a strike when he generously donated: "He went two [or three] consecutive in a row." You can say that again; but I guess you did, did. . . .

I know I'm making inroads on pleonasms. The other day I found the written graffiti "Trust me on this one, pleonasms are a risky gamble." . . . And this was in the faculty washroom! . . . in crayon!

And speaking of delicate balances, friendly smiles, wooden planks, green grass, positive congratulations, painful hurts, and downtown center city (did you pick up the recurring pattern?), are you negatively troubled by such pleonastic expressions as hand gloves? widow woman? long length? college professor? small compact cars? someone's own self-admission? small gnats? and whoever that guy is from Down Under? Oh, truly really? Not me! It's *your* baggage to hand-carry from now on! This is where I get off, leaving you to hold this particular bag.

But however, so long as you are going to be my verbal red cap, may I ask you to please give thoughtful consideration to giving a contributed (pleonastic) donation by way of the structured form on page 95. Psychologically, I'm a big tipper.

## PLEONASMS, UNCLASSIFIED: PRICELESS FREE GIFTS I HAVE KNOWN AND/OR LOVED

For a beginning premise, as every grown adult knows, and at the risk of attracting a large crowd, I would like to return back again to the original initial first title name of this published book (before my demanding editor did her thing), i.e., *Free Gift*.

Nevertheless in spite of that, not to make this a long speech, I was recently sadly appalled to hear a story about an ordained minister, a wandering vagabond, a singing troubadour, and a homeless streetperson who were stranded in Plano, Texas. Presumably, one was an indigenous native, a rural farmer, alone by himself. I forget the remaining rest of this forgettable story.

See if, in your subjective judgment, you think the following pleonasms are a perfect fit, or even a good bargain:

simian monkey
synthetic substitute
identified target
computer technology
dead corpse
male bull
duplicate copy
erotic pornography
negative reaction
bright yellow
dull economics
dull economics (real fact, real fact)
dull statistics
hard work
senior executive
urbane sophisticate (which reminds me of my memorable not-
to-be-forgotten Plano, Texas story)
special uniqueness

Regarding the Iran-contra hearings, on the pleonastic side of the aisle, consider contra rebel, communist Sandinistas, contra war, high mountain, humanitarian aid, and anti-contra. (P.S. Don't repeat these pleonasms.) (P.P.S. Don't repeat these pleonasms.)

I saw some more written graffiti the other day: "If old novel is an oxymoron, new novel is a pleonasm." It was written in plaid sprayed spray paint . . . on what had formerly used to be an empty void.

I'm certainly sure I don't know about you, but I get anxiously uneasy whenever I see the local bank sign "Fidelity Trust." I mean, would you trust your cash money, accumulated savings, positive assets, to an organization with a pleonasm for a name?

On a strangely bizarre story on the one-hour show *60 Minutes*, well-renowned Mayor Edward Koch of New York, New York, talked about a family relative. Well, I suppose if you have to have relatives (even in New York, New York) . . .

I still continue to take the following old clichés to be repeatable pleonasms:

free choice
hot steam
bad war
left-handed southpaw (Right on!)
rural farmer
disposable garbage
serious danger
moral honesty
dangerous threat
final results

But then, maybe I just don't understand exactly.

Also too, it has been reportedly said I've been described as being consistently dependable, which is a positive improvement on being described as being consistently reliable, which, you will recall again, is fundamentally basic in becoming a mature adult.

On playing sports: Verne Lundquist, during the January 1988 Purdue–Louisville basketball game, described Purdue as having a "tenacious sticky defense." (So *that's* what the big black P on the yellow flag stands for!) Hang and/or adhere in there, Verne.

Who was it who not too long ago recently described someone as being a grotesque monster? A macho man I can understand, or someone with manly virility, or a royal king, or even a famous celebrity, but a grotesque monster? C'mon!

And, not totally unrelated, Mike Tyson described himself as having fought an "intelligent fight." Pleonasm? Or oxymoron? Anything you say, Mike, I hasten to add—quickly.

**Microdot
(illustrated with the
assistance of the author)**

And how many times have you heard:

Here he is himself.
major significance
two-point safety
good manners
efficient productivity
mean average

And on another news radio broadcast, I surely certainly heard high-level waste (right, high-level waste is an oxymoron; I just wanted to see if you were actively alert), fragile eggshell, intoxicated drunk, government regulation, funny comedian, fast acceleration (which potentially probably beats slow braking), cynical iconoclast (my kind of guy! As a matter of fact, when I was a young kid growing up, all my idols were iconoclasts), fat pork, political compromise, and (hold onto your whatever) a porous screen?—the final latter being a totally solid pleonasm.

With acquiescent agreement, I would allow that a porous screen is to be positively preferred to an empty hole, an open door, an open conduit, an empty space, and an open field, and even an old classic. (You're right, old classic has nothing to do with the rest of those pleonasms; it's of a different genre type altogether. Hey, you *are* listening!) I just wanted to see if you were listening. (I said, I just wanted to see if you were listening!)

Tell me again, which one of the presidential candidates was it who was described as being the people's populist?

(I really don't mind being alone; I just hate losing those arguments—decisively.)

And, in ultimate finality, my hopeful preference is that you could indeed distinguish these

Unclassified pleonasms from the Miscellaneous pleonasms and the Other pleonasms. If you could, you are to be positively commended (and seriously mistrusted). If you couldn't, it is maybe probably either a character flaw or a character strength—yours, not mine. I have none. In either case, however, you certainly definitely will want to specifically identify yourself by taking positive advantage of (what else?) the explanations on the self-explanatory form on page 95. Gotcha! I would read the self-explanatory instructions to you, but . . .

**Rigid stubbornness**

# 8 My Ten Favorite Pleonasms: My Ten Favorite Pleonasms

Unlike my fixed position on my ten favorite oxymorons, I wish someone *would* ask me my ten favorite pleonasms. Let me say that again, I wish someone *would* ask me my ten favorite pleonasms.

I thought you would never ask. Following, in systematic order, are my ten favorite pleonasms:

microdot
free gift
subjective rating
repeated redundancy
free gift
miscellaneous other
exact same
cash money
microdot
final conclusion

I *told* you they were redundant, repeatedly.

# 9
# Live Evil:
# Approximately 101 Palindromes Run Amok

This is the high-tech section of the book. Welcome to programmed instruction, folks. Here's the way it operates:

(A) *If* you perceive yourself as an oxymoron addict, begin with the next section. (2) *If* you perceive yourself as a pleonasm addict, skip the next section and begin with the one after that. (iii) *If* you perceive yourself as *both* an oxymoron addict *and* a pleonasm addict, begin with both sections (simultaneously), take two aspirins, and call yourself in the morning—just be careful what you call yourself. Or (d) if you perceive yourself as *neither* an oxymoron addict *nor* a pleonasm addict (inconceivable!), skip both sections (in any order) and go directly to Boardwalk via square one—pass beyond.

Something for almost everyone!

## A. The Next Section (for Oxymoron Addicts Only)

In a lengthy moment of mild strength (my editor's, not mine), I sort of committed myself to include a third word type—palindromes. As is not the case with oxymorons and pleonasms, which no one ever heard of (or, for you purists, of which no one ever heard), everyone in the world knows what palindromes are. (The reason I am pausing here is that my train of thought has been interrupted by what can be described only as a great national gnashing of teeth. I remain unafraid, inasmuch as, to my faulty knowledge, no one has ever been gummed to death—although it doesn't sound that unpleasant.)

For that single (or married) unknowing individual, whosoever he/she may be (how's that for sensitivity? Who said I ain't got no class?), let the record indicate palindromes are words, phrases, or sentences spelled the same forward as backward. They are symmetrical expressions, mirror images—expressions spelled (and occasionally pronounced) the same whether you move left to right *or* right to left. At this point, given that you are a self-confessed oxymoron junkie, I am tempted to comment "same difference" (but I will successfully resist that temptation). However, we are now briefly in palindromes—on the level. (Hey, right, *level* is a . . .)

### (2) The One After That (for Pleonasm Addicts Only)

In a brief moment of powerful strength (my editor's not mine), I staunchly committed myself to include a third word type—palindromes. As is not the case with oxymorons and pleonasms, which no one ever heard of (or, for you purists, of which no one ever heard), everyone in the world knows what palindromes are. (The reason I am pausing here is that my train of thought has been interrupted by what can be described only as a great national gnashing of teeth. I remain unafraid, inasmuch as, to my factual knowledge, no one has ever been gummed to death—although it doesn't sound that unpleasant.)

For that single (or married) unknowing individual, whosoever she/he may be (how's that for sensitivity? Who said I ain't got no class?), let the record indicate palindromes are words, phrases, or sentences spelled the same forward as backward. They are symmetrical expressions, mirror images—expressions spelled (and occasionally pronounced) the exact same whether you move left to right *or* right to left. At this point, given that you are a pleonasm junkie, I am tempted to comment "middle center" (but I will successfully resist that temptation). However, we are now briefly in palindromes—on the level. (Hey, right, *level* is a . . .)

**(iii)** (For Oxymoron *and* Pleonasm Addicts Only)

See (A) and (2) above.


**(d)** (For *Neither* Oxymoron *nor* Pleonasm Addicts Only)

Seek professional help, now, quickly.


## Pronunciation

So much for definition; and given my track record for pronunciation, I'm going to leave it up to you on this one. It will be easier for all of us that way. Following are some palindromic droppings (and I choose my words and my readers, if not my friends, carefully).


## Palindromes Away!

At noon, as Mom, Dad, Sis, Bob, Nan, Ara, Abba, Asa, Otto, Eve, and the twins, Anna and Lil, and I sat around discussing this palindromic chapter, I said, "Aha, and/or wow, Pop, this palindromic chapter is going to be a short one, inasmuch as I seem to have misplaced my palindromic chapter file." (As a matter of fact, I really couldn't find the file until about 10:01 [our time]. However, as you know, when you lose things, they are always in the last place you look. Therefore, the best thing to do is look in the last place first.)

Anyway, later that day, on the eve of this gig, having parked my Civic, stashed my kayak, removed my gag, checked the radar, greeted the nun (she concerned about live evil), performed my solos (without a peep, I might add), I found my pip of a palindrome file. Then, after securing the bib on Bob, Nan and the pup (to say naught of the ewe [I always say if you can't say something naught, don't say nothing at all]) performed their swap-paws trick.

Not to be outdone, Otto (which you will recall is *toot* spelled inside out), who is no boob, gave us the straight poop—with pep (as opposed to pap). At this point, looking me in the eye, my pop said, "No, son. Tut, tut; don't concern yourself about palindromes. Just tell your ogre [he always mispronounces "editor"—maybe it's hereditary] they don't exist; you made the whole thing up. Either that or tell her you couldn't come up with any." Wow! (Or, as we are wont to say in Atlanta, Wow!) Tit for tat.

The other advice he gave me was "Step on no pets." (I've always tried to live my life by that credo.) "But, Dad," I protested weakly, sometimes daily (whoops, those are homophones—stop me before I learn anything else), "that's a palindromic phrase." To which he replied sagely, "Okay, so I lied."

### They're Here

Palindromes, unlike oxymorons and those other things (y'know, the P word), are *not* ubiquitous (just insidious)—they *are* difficult to find (or haven't you noticed?). However, once awareness has been heightened, it is not so difficult to perceive yourself as the victim of a semantic conspiracy.

For example, my office zip code is 30303; my late Aunt Devera and Uncle Jack lived in apartment 303; my digital Mickey Mouse watch yields readings of 12:21, 10:01, and 11:11. I recently flew on a 707 (or was it a 727, 737, 747, or 757? . . . or 767? or did I get that backward?).

The Atlanta area code is 404; the area code of my editor (am I pronouncing that correctly, Dad?) is 212; and if I want to call colleagues in Honolulu, Santa Rosa, Denver, Washington, D.C.,

Lexington, Albuquerque, Raleigh, Detroit, Harrisburg, Des Moines, and/or Milwaukee, more of the same—from either direction.

Speaking of colleagues, I recently received my professional dues statement from the American Psychological Association (right! APA!). Could have been worse; I used to be a member of the American Statistical Association (right! . . . ). And wow! I think my Dad may still yet continue to be a member of the American Dental Association (do you suppose it's hereditary?).

When I was a second lieutenant (I had to be an officer—I was too young to be an enlisted man), some of the military times were temporal palindromes—1001, 1111, 1221, 1331, 1441, 1551, 2222, and 2332—not that it helped. But it couldn't hurt. (Even then, though not realizing it, I was already into pleonasms, using time terms such as 1001AM or 1111AM or 1221PM or 1331PM or 1441PM or 1551PM or 2222PM or 2332PM.)

## Le Grand Gotcha

Incidentally, now that *you're* into palindromes (or is it the other way around?), you might find it of momentary moment to go back through this book and see if you can find all the palindromes that *got by you* the first time. (Aha! Le Grand Gotcha!)

On the other hand, you might find simultaneous root canal work and IRS audit—without benefit of an anesthetic—almost as much fun. No choice (he said oxymoronically), heh, heh, heh.

## Other: Wait, There's More!

I have a colleague here at the university (would that I had more than *a* colleague here at the university) who tells me the classic palindrome is Able was I ere I saw Elba. I didn't know Napoleon was into palindromes—as well as brandy and pastries.

And, for both sexes, consider the palindromic Madam, I'm Adam.

Or, Rise to vote, sir.

That colleague also tells me, as we presumably prepare to give up our rights to the Panama Canal, we should remember President Theodore Roosevelt ostensibly said—or at least inferred—the dramatic palindromatic "A man, a plan, a canal—Panama!" Hey, palindromatically, it makes sense to me—whether you enter and/or leave from the Pacific side and/or the Atlantic side.

**Pals slap**

Have you noticed how athletic teammates give high fives? . . . I suppose you could say pals slap. Huh?

I saw some interesting palindromic graffiti recently on a hospital operating-room wall: "Nurses run." (Presumably the surgical staff could only blunt with "We sew.") So?

Some kook recently suggested that we might repaper our offices in a redder color. Hah!

And perhaps it was Sir Winston Churchill (or Soupy Sales) who might have said, "Now, sir, a war is won." Okay, so it wasn't Sir Winston Churchill (or Soupy Sales)—but it *could* have been! Oscar Wilde? You're kidding! Believe me, that's incredible.

My understanding is that there is an Iranian history book the title of which is *Shahs*.

Can you find the palindrome below?

rotor

Close enough!


## SOS

Well, that demonstrates I couldn't think of any palindromes. But how did *you* do? Go ahead; toot (which, you will recall, is *Otto* spelled inside out) your own horn. We're going to have to drop this particular chapter. (Alas, Mom and Dad, a dud deed). Aha! Perhaps it is not too late to send out an SOS.

And speaking of SOS (the distress signal, not the delightful military breakfast treat), take a peep at the mailer on page 95 ere you begin the final assault on the following semantic molehill— the dreaded mighty (or is it mighty dreaded?) combination oxymorons and pleonasms (hold the palindromes) chapter. Hey, I deliver, huh?

# 10 The Dual Curse: A Normal Routine Whole Half-Day with an Oxymoron and/or Pleonasm Addict

More and more, less and less, I more or less realize I am seemingly almost inextricably totally completely hooked on oxymorons and/or pleonasms—I forget which (or is it the opposite?). And like all good addicts, I am convinced I can kick the habit, control my life, do whatever I want—whenever I want. (But who wants?)

Therefore, on a recent Sunday, approximately January 10, 1988, rather than work on this small large project (or is it a large small project?), I decided to spend an entire whole half-day watching NFL professional football playoff football games . . . just to get away for a day, as well as prepare for Super Bowl XXII. (Although, self-admittedly, I could have settled for the Thursday Night Edition of *Monday Night Football*.)

So therefore, thus predisposed, I kissed my family (or whoever those people were) good-bye, sent them off to the longest triple feature I could find (*Lawrence of Arabia* was the selected short subject), closed shut (and bolted) the door, settled into the couch (the one-seater) in front of my black-and-black permanent portable air-cooled steam-operated television set—hoping for the best. But it was not to be.

It didn't work. No contest. Soon the addiction(s) took over; and I was taking copious notes. Forgive me (or not), but the following is what I picked up—or was it the other way around?

## Chicago Bears Versus Washington Redskins: Game I

The game was reported by reporters Pat Summerall and John Madden, and I won't even discuss their discussion of three ends—clearly an oxymoron (the mind, not to mention geometry and anatomy, boggles—three? That's almost as tough as imagining a piece of rope so long it only has one end [again], or imagining the sound of one hand clapping [again], or imagining my new electric gravity-operated one-way pendulum).

A few pleonasms turned up early: graceful athlete, cat quick, Payton run, aggressive tackle, hard tackle, fair referee . . . and who could ever forget, uh, uh, quick sprint? Later, Summerall talked about the open hole, as well as the large crowd. I was also particularly struck by someone's discussion of a big 300-pounder (as distinguished, I suppose, from a small 300-pounder). On further thought, I only assumed they spoke of a player. Possibly they were describing a fast food new innovation.

Lest you think all I heard was pleonasms, consider football play. Also, Madden said (I think, how can you tell?), "You *know* Mike Ditka is upset—he stays that way." Is that consistent status quo? Consistent change? Changing status quo? More important, is it possible?

Not to be given to excessive overreaction, Madden (perhaps in an attempted try to make up in some small subtle way for the three-ends paradox) handed off the oxymoronic "Bears have both ends on the same side." (Hey, now we're getting somewhere. Those guys are really built, sorta.) That *has* to be painful—or at least inconvenient, like for example in the woods.

Someone talked about frozen ice (that's the best kind—if you can just remember the formula), as well as positive advantage—although the other dynamic-dyad half, not to be overly outdone, countered with positive disadvantage. There was also some talk of clock time—again, one of my timeless timely favorites (although in all partial complete candor, it used to tick me off). On that score, did I tell you about my digital Mickey Mouse watch? (Okay, so Mickey is slightly psychotic; but what would you expect of an intensely compulsive hand watcher?!)

When the propitious moment arrived (and it always seems to come at just the right time), there was discussion of "their second first down." If only . . .

I'm not sure, but I think someone talked about an even tie at one point (although I personally felt the game was even closer than the score suggested).

About the time I was beginning to think CBS Sports may be a pleonastic oxymoron (official time out!), someone put forth the pleonasm high pressure—which I suppose is better than the oxymoron low pressure. Madden suggested one team was going to press tight. That's almost certainly the best way; to press loose would be an oxymoron (but of course the defensive coaching staff knew that; that's why they're paid [cash money] to be defensive coaches).

Summerall, not to be outdone, talked about the up back, as well as the safety blitz, as well as the punt return (oxymorons and/or pleonasms? You pick 'em!).

Mr. Madden, to show demonstrably he can go both ways, sometimes simultaneously, offered the thoughtful pleonasm "At one time, you couldn't hurdle over a tackler." That got a rise out of me. I confess I admit I am not very tough; so I don't know whether painful injury is an oxymoron or a pleonasm—unless, of course, it hurts so good (or the other). But I do think down lineman is a pleonasm.

After later, someone said the temperature was in the high teens. Ice freezes at such high low temperatures—unless you bring it inside.

Later on, Madden oxymoronically offered "I kind of agree with the fans." Hey, so long as you're sorta sure. Not to be semantically squashed, he also offered "You can't keep going to the well with the same thing." (Any takers?)

Other oxymorons turned up at about this point: placement kicker, right tackle, and "They came up with the same playback the other way." (Credit Summerall with this off-tackle oxymoron.) Hey, same difference.

Then, biff, boff, and/or doink, came a series of pleonasms: bare skin, short pause, fiercely competitive. Mercy, please! This repeated but redundant pleonastic outpouring was followed by a fairly lengthy skein of oxymorons (all in a row), to include "had it momentarily," "no time," and "He made that incompletion." (You think that last one is easy? You have to catch it, drop it, catch it, drop it, ca . . .)

Somebody, I'm not sure to whom to give the grudging credit, came up with the all-time semi-classic pleonasm: young rookie. Agelessly evergreen! No doubt yon young rookie had been taught a few things by the wily old veteran. Let's hear it for clichés—old and new!

And then, biff, doink, and/or bang, came "spin around."

Then, almost instant relief (a commercial from Subaru), but no. They contributed to my addiction, poured fire on the fool, with the old traditional classic "The more things change, the more they stay the same." I always thought so; but then I changed my mind. Think so?

Then the game turned around; the oxymorons actually really took the upper hand. (Upper hand? Built like that, you're almost bound to attract attention when you and your date walk in the drive-through window at your local fast food gourmet franchise.) I heard forward lateral (how I hoped I could have also heard backward lateral, just to even things out). But no, Summerall pleonastically came up with falling down. Had only the player fallen up, he might have attained sainthood (outside of New Orleans) or, better, the NFL Follies (you tell me if that's an oxymoron or a pleonasm!).

Another commercial break, during which Subaru struck again with "inexpensive car." (. . . and I have the cashed, cancelled check to almost prove it).

As I was trying to decide whether "out of time-outs" was an oxymoron or a pleonasm (let alone how one handles the plural form of *time-out* without offending the rabid fans, or, you purists), one of the players received an "outstanding tribute" from the very same rabid fans. I suppose he was deserving (how quickly they remember).

Just when the pleonasms seemed to be slowly creeping into the lead, the oxymorons struck back. With 1:10 minutes left in the game came: "One or two more last chances may remain."

While I was deciding if fumble recovery qualified as an oxymoron, the Bears came up to their last fourth down. As we all know, the game ended in "a bitter defeat for the Bears." Do you think they could live with a pyrrhic victory in Chicago? Huh?

The Redskins were described as the "winning victors." Yet once again, if you have to be a winner (or victor), that's the best way to be.

I'm confidently certain you'll agree the most fantastic unusual part of the whole afternoon was that *not once* (really!) did Summerall, *or* Madden, verbally mention the words "oxymoron" *or* "pleonasm." No, I'm serious.

**Offensive-tackle**

## Houston Oilers Versus Denver Broncos: Game II

Although I was self-admittedly excitedly exhausted pleonastically and oxymoronically, neither Dick Enberg nor Merlin Olsen had yet begun to give contributions—although I can visually picture them coolly warming up somewhere off camera. If my perceptions of their donated contributions seem briefer than for those of Game I, it is only because I was dizzily groggy from Game I. By the time Game II started, I was somewhat satiated, had writer's cramp, and was clearly confused.

Notwithstanding though, here are but a few from that very heatedly contested competition (a potential quadruple—and in the pike position! Them pikes really know how to live!). I'm tired, *you* tell me into which category they fall (or, for you real true purists, which category they fall in, to): physically aggressive, immediate rush, solid screen, cool heat, a whole gang, and standing still. How did you do? Well, maybe next time; try to persevere harder.

Almost suddenly, I had a new idea—again. These renowned celebrities were generous contributors to my solid pool (or, less accurately, clear morass). For example, Olsen offered the pleonasm "These subtle little moves set up the offense." Darn, and I missed it! Later, there was an illegal foul. Those, presumably, are worse than the legal fouls. I also think I heard middle center, which I certainly hope so.

I know I heard bad injury. While I wish no one ill, I would agree good injuries are to be preferred. Fortunately luckily, no one was hurt bad.

Pleonastically, Enberg also gave us "The team needs desperately to score." Gosh, who doesn't?

I'm not sure how to classify Olsen's "on both sides of the ball," particularly since it was not a round ball. I also might have heard close proximity—which is again to be nearly preferred to distant proximity. Olsen's "other key" also desires something to be left.

Pleonasms came back into play when they talked about a shrill whistle. As I always say (and sometimes at the most embarrassingly appropriate times), shrill is as shrill does.

At about this point, I was ready to change my mind about whether dry martini was a pleonasm or an oxymoron. And as I somewhat accurately recollect, I did so, several times. Fortunately, I forget from which position I was changing, changing, changing. . . .

Not to worry, Enberg delivered the oxymoron, missed assignment—either an anticipated and/or unanticipated expectation. Then we got shortcut (you tell me).

How about rule change? Too smart? Credit Enberg with the first former and credit Olsen with the second latter. And the former also generously donated the contribution "Everything worked well for the Broncos." Let's hear it for the pleonasms. Rah, Rah (and Rah—but not necessarily in that sequential order).

**Gourmet hot dogs**

At this point, I took the third quarter off to have dinner—consisting primarily of gourmet hot dogs, one of my live-in wife's best (un)intentional recipes. What else could I do? We were all out of caviar helper. (Actually I shouldn't tease her [who's teasing?] about her cooking and/or recipes, so-called—although I think it is of moment to point out during the first few decades of our wedded marriage, most recipes called for a teaspoon of Unguentine. Potholders were like putty in her hands. She treated me like a minor deity, often putting burnt offerings before me—but never after me.)

Also, about this point, I heard highest standards on a Pennzoil ad, as well as high-performance luxury on a Mazda ad. Have you noticed how commercials are becoming increasingly oxymoronic—new, improved?

The way the game went, I finally gave up . . . partly totally accepting Houston offense as an oxymoron and Denver defense as a pleonasm. I'm looking forward to my next visit to Denver—and also to my last visit to Houston.

But the whole half-day wasn't a complete total productive waste in terms of my first original goal of preparing for Super Bowl XXII. I believe I'm almost totally ready; I can't wait to see who wins: the Oxymoron Female Rams (whose semiofficial team colors are bright gray, subtle red for the trim, with solid plaid accents) *or* the Pleonasm Tiger Cats (whose extremely official team colors are dark black, dark black for the trim, with dark black accents). Both teams may be overmatched, but neither will be overdressed.

My pick? I plan to root intensely for both teams (that way I won't be disappointed).

At this point, my family (or whoever those people were) returned, having survived the movie films and the stale popcorn (I wonder . . .). Sensing my tired fatigue, in a purposeful effort to get my mind off television, they suggested we talk about oxymorons and/or pleonasms.

Gnash, gnash; let's hear it for domestic violence; it's okay to tell.

# Conclusions:
## Interim and/or Final Poop

Well, you were warned on page 20 that I'd be back to meet you after you had tramped through the oxymoronic/pleonastic/palindromic woods. And sure enough, here I am, almost. How did you do? More important, how did *I* do? Can we still be friends? . . . friendly enemies? Oh, yeah? Same to you, fella! Oh, pardon me, madam.

### Complete Partial Truth (or at Least a Cease-Fire)

In the few remaining pages, I really seriously want to address two socially meaningful questions that have plagued thinkers, seekers of truth, and other troublemakers throughout the ages. The first is: "Can a girl with a mole love a gopher (and find happiness in a small mining town in Montana)?" And the second—as posed in *Jumbo Shrimp*—is: "What does it all mean?"

The more important first question I will leave to the philosophers, cab drivers, sages, and bartenders who have wrestled with that question since trees began falling in noisy forests—but *not* in oxymoronic/pleonastic/palindromic woods. Rather, I will address my almost complete attention to the less important second question; because, to be somewhat candid, I'd kinda like to know myself . . . what *does* it all mean?

## What does it all mean?

    **(a)** no conclusion
    **(b)** two diametrically opposing—but equally correct—conclusions

**(c)** to be continued
**(d)** all of the above

The keyed correct response is *either* (a), (b), *and* (c) . . . *or* (d). How did you do? But let me explain, barely, but briefly. Simply basically, the answer clearly is everything . . . and nothing . . . and everything . . . and . . .

And having now read the re-revealed answer to the age-old question, you can either drop out of the long march here or still continue on. However, it is mandatory you yourself make the optional choice, now.

## Now What?

Perhaps not unlike you (and my editor), I can't wait to see how and/or how soon and/or if this all ends. I'll bet you can't figure out how I'm going to tie all this together. Neither can I (but there are still a few pages left) . . . although I have to be honest with you, I'm seriously considering (to be continued). But first . . .

## Testy Test: I Give Up; What Is It, Oxymoron or Pleonasm?

Certainly not unlike you, I'm not particularly good at games and stuff like that. As a matter of fact, I was recently stymied (temporarily) by a puzzle that directed me to "connect the dot." (Actually, it wasn't all that difficult. I got it right . . . the second time . . . without much help.)

Notwithstanding, I think the time has come to assess *your* mastery of this mystery. Below are thirty-one expressions. Your assignment, should you choose to accept it, is to decide whether the

**Crowded sky**

expressions are oxymorons *or* pleonasms. Score yourself (but not badly); I trust you (what choice do I have?). Incidentally, should you need it, the key appears on page 99. Do *not* peek. (I *asked* you not to peek . . . gotcha!)

1. upside-down logic
2. foreign alien
3. healthy tan
4. hot chili
5. intelligent fight
6. personal computer
7. true love
8. resident alien
9. criminal lawyer
10. Batman's actual secret true identity
11. true sincerity
12. natural grass
13. NFL Follies
14. greater good
15. false sincerity
16. measured meter
17. Otto (or toot)

18. shortcut
19. lesser evil
20. relentlessly continued
21. "my other brother Darryl."
    (I used to have trouble keeping them separate—but then it came to me: Darryl is the taller—or is it the shorter?—of the two.)
22. domestic import
23. de-install
24. natural gas
25. Ms. America Beauty Contest
26. toot (or Otto)
27. meatloaf surprise
28. crowded sky
29. still life
30. American English
31. good sex

*How to score yourself:* (1) Stand on one foot (minimum) while humming the haunting theme from *Mr. Ed* in three-part harmony. (2) Record how many items you got totally correct or partly correct, giving yourself 1 point for each. (3) Record how many items you got totally wrong or partly wrong, giving yourself 1 point for each. (4) Finally (or midtermly), add up your two scores, together.

If you attempted all items and got a score of 31, you are to be commended. But—and this is important—on the other hand, if you attempted all items and got a score of less than 31, you are to be commended (and you should check your arithmetic).

How did you do? Very extremely fairly good; I'm impressed.

### Now What? Is There Partial Life After Oxymorons? Is There Vital Life After Pleonasms?

Yes, almost, and more than.

Having settled that, let me make a few comments regarding personal goals and observations.

As indicated in the introduction (as well as in *Jumbo Shrimp)*, perhaps my original goals were a little much (or perhaps even a little more than much). Oh, sure, I did eventually indeed become an internationally unknown oxymoron expert, a nameless celebrity, an instant folk hero, an academic sex symbol, an oxymoron club franchiser, a T-shirt designer, and modestly famous (but that's 211 history—right?—current, ancient, old, and/or modern.)

Essentially true enough, I failed badly to become the consummate ultimate antepenultimist, as well as the consummate ultimate anti-antepenultimist. However, it may not be too late—although certainly the competition still continues to be keen (but I've never shied away from a challenge before—unless, of course, I felt threatened).

**Upside-down logic**

### The Past Lies Behind, But the Future Lies Ahead

On the other hand, I have now accomplished my former life's goal of ruining your life by way of oxymoron addiction, as well as now having accomplished my current life's goal of ruining your life by way of pleonasm addiction. What greater legacy can a person leave, behind?

In regard to oxymorons, I intend to continue to be a semantic pusher, hanging around playgrounds and libraries, pulling unsuspecting kids aside and saying, "Hey, kid, want to try an oxymoron?" In regard to pleonasms, I plan to become a semantic exorcist, driving out the repeatedly redundant. No, I really do truly seriously honestly intend to plan to continue to still exorcise out this (semantically speaking) diabolical devil.

And palindromes? Well, they really don't exist; never did; never will. I made that pup up. You don't really believe there is any such word as *palindrome*, do you? . . .

. . . any more than there are words like *oxymoron* or *pleonasm?* (Le Grander Gotcha.)

And please pronounce at least one of the three words (you do remember the three words, don't you?) correctly. . . . Correct misspelling and/or incorrect mispelling is/are optional.

*Caveat emptor,* y'all!

(*Now* can I get back to being an industrial-organizational psychologist again? and/or [to be continued], he said ominously).

This is the last word (and *I* got it). Right?

# MAILER: Third Deadline, Absolute Deadline

Once again, had enough? Once again, can't stand it any longer? Then once again, grasp pen between thumb and forefinger. Complete the following and mail to:

**Dr. Warren S. Blumenfeld**
**Internationally Unknown Oxymoron Expert & Well-Renowned Pleonasm Authority**
**The Oxymoron (& Pleonasm) (& Palindrome) Institute of North America (and Georgia)**
**International Worldwide Headquarters (Home Office)**
**PO Box 824003**
**Atlanta, GA 30324**
**Attention: *Jumbo Shrimp/Pretty Ugly* New Improved Products Division**

My favorite oxymoron was _____

My favorite pleonasm was _____

My favorite palindrome was _____

Ten oxymorons, pleonasms, and/or palindromes that were not included, but should have been, and probably will be in the next book are:

| OXYMORON/PLEONASM/PALINDROME | SOURCE |
| --- | --- |
| 1. _____ | _____ |
| 2. _____ | _____ |
| 3. _____ | _____ |
| 4. _____ | _____ |

5. _____

6. _____

7. _____

8. _____

9. _____

etc. _____

My name is _____

My address is _____

_____

I probably will definitely buy one or more copies of the next oxymoron book:

_____ Maybe       _____ Firmest maybe

_____ Firm maybe       _____ Qualified maybe (Be less specific, if at all possible, please.)

_____ Firmer maybe

I will absolutely positively buy several multiple copies of the next forthcoming published pleonasm book:

_____ For sure       _____ Absolutely for sure

_____ Certainly for sure       _____ Guaranteed for sure (Be more specific if at all possible, please.)

_____ Positively for sure

Thank you for your interest, apathetic and/or intense.

And all together now, let's hear it for anarchy and unanonymity—as well as for oxymorons and pleonasms, . . . okay, and palindromes!